D0724419

Vocabulary Power Plus
for the ACT

Vocabulary,
Reading, and Writing
Exercises for High Scores

Level Twelve

By Daniel A. Reed

Edited by Paul Moliken

Prestwick House

P.O. Box 658 • Clayton, DE 19938
(800) 932-4593 • www.prestwickhouse.com

ISBN   978-1-935467-08-3

Copyright ©2011 by Prestwick House, Inc.
All rights reserved. No portion may be
reproduced without permission in writing
from the publisher. Revised February 2012.

Level Twelve

Vocabulary Power Plus for the ACT

Vocabulary,
Reading, and Writing
Exercises for High Scores

•*Table of Contents* •

Vocabulary
Power Plus
for the **ACT**
Vocabulary,
Reading, and Writing
Exercises for High Scores

·Introduction·

VOCABULARY POWER PLUS FOR THE ACT combines classroom tested vocabulary drills with reading and writing exercises designed to prepare students for the American College Testing assessment; however, *Vocabulary Power Plus for the ACT* is a resource for all students—not just those who are college bound or preparing for the ACT. This series is intended to increase vocabulary, improve grammar, enhance writing, and boost critical reading skills for students at all levels of learning.

Vocabulary lessons combine words-in-context exercises with inferences to ensure that definitions are understood, instead of merely memorized.

Lengthy critical reading exercises and detailed questions emulate the reading passages of the ACT Reading test. Each passage involves a topic in social studies, natural science, prose fiction, or humanities, and is accompanied by multiple levels of questions.

ACT-style grammar passages and questions provide practice in punctuation, usage, structure, and word choice.

The process-oriented writing exercises in *Vocabulary Power Plus for the ACT* develop speed and thrift in essay writing, qualifiable with the objective writing fundamentals in the simulated ACT essay scoring guide.

We hope that you find the *Vocabulary Power Plus for the ACT* series to be an effective tool for teaching new words and an exceptional tool for preparing for the ACT.

Strategies for Completing Activities

Roots, Prefixes, and Suffixes

A knowledge of roots, prefixes, and suffixes can give readers the ability to view unfamiliar words as puzzles that require only a few simple steps to solve. For the person interested in the history of words, this knowledge provides the ability to track word origin and evolution. For those who seek to improve vocabulary, this knowledge creates a sure and lifelong method; however, there are two points to remember:

1. Some words have evolved through usage, so present definitions might differ from what you infer through an examination of the roots and prefixes. The word *abstruse*, for example, contains the prefix *ab* (away) and the root *trudere* (to thrust), and literally means *to thrust away*. Today, *abstruse* is used to describe something that is hard to understand.

2. Certain roots do not apply to all words that use the same form. If you know that the root *vin* means "to conquer," then you would be correct in concluding that the word *invincible* means "incapable of being conquered"; however, if you tried to apply the same root meaning to *vindicate* or *vindictive*, you would be incorrect. When analyzing unfamiliar words, check for other possible roots if your inferred meaning does not fit the context.

Despite these considerations, a knowledge of roots and prefixes is one of the best ways to build a powerful vocabulary.

Critical Reading

Reading questions generally fall into several categories.

1. *Identifying the main idea or the author's purpose.* Generally, the question will ask, "What is this selection about?"

In some passages, the author's purpose will be easy to identify because one or two ideas leap from the text; however, other passages might not be so easily analyzed, especially if they include convoluted sentences. Inverted sentences (subject at the end of the sentence) and elliptical sentences (words missing) will also increase the difficulty of the passages, but all of these obstacles can be overcome if readers take one sentence at a time and recast it in their own words. Consider the following sentence:

These writers either jot down their thoughts bit by bit, in short, ambiguous, and paradoxical sentences, which apparently mean much more than they say—of this kind of writing Schelling's treatises on natural philosophy are a splendid instance; or else they hold forth with a deluge of words and the most intolerable diffusiveness, as though no end of fuss were necessary to make the reader understand the deep meaning of their sentences, whereas it is some quite simple if not actually trivial idea, examples of which may be found in plenty in the popular works of Fichte, and the philosophical manuals of a hundred other miserable dunces.

If we edit out some of the words, the main point of this sentence is obvious.

These writers either jot down their thoughts bit by bit, in short, sentences, which apparently mean much more than they say

or

they hold a deluge of words

as though necessary to make the reader understand the deep meaning of their sentences

Some sentences need only a few deletions for clarification, but others require major recasting and additions; they must be read carefully and put into the reader's own words.

Some in their discourse desire rather commendation of wit, in being able to hold all arguments, than of judgment, in discerning what is true; as if it were a praise to know what might be said, and not what should be thought.

After studying it, a reader might recast the sentence as follows:

In conversation, some people desire praise for their abilities to maintain the conversation rather than for their abilities to identify what is true or false, as though it were better to sound good than to know what is truth or fiction.

2. Identifying the stated or implied meaning. *What is the author stating or suggesting?*

The literal meaning of a text does not always correspond with the intended meaning. To understand a passage fully, readers must determine which meaning—if there is more than one—is the intended meaning of the passage.

Consider the following sentence:

> If his notice was sought, an expression of courtesy and interest gleamed out upon his features; proving that there was light within him and that it was only the outward medium of the intellectual lamp that obstructed the rays in their passage.

Interpreted literally, this Nathaniel Hawthorne metaphor suggests that a light-generating lamp exists inside of the human body. Since this is impossible, the reader must look to the metaphoric meaning of the passage to properly understand it. In the metaphor, Hawthorne refers to the human mind—consciousness—as a lamp that emits light, and other people cannot always see the lamp because the outside "medium"—the human body—sometimes blocks it.

3. Identifying the tone or mood of the selection. *What feeling does the text evoke?*

To answer these types of questions, readers must look closely at individual words and their connotations; for example, the words *stubborn* and *firm* have almost the same definition, but a writer who describes a character as *stubborn* rather than *firm* is probably suggesting something negative about the character.

Writing

The ACT writing exam allocates only thirty minutes to the composition of a well-organized, fully developed essay. Writing a satisfactory essay in this limited time requires the ability to quickly determine a thesis, organize ideas, and produce adequate examples to support the ideas.

An essay written in thirty minutes might not represent the best process writing—an ACT essay might lack the perfection and depth that weeks of proofreading and editing give to research papers. Process is undoubtedly important, but students must consider the time constraints of the ACT. Completion of the essay is just as important as organization, development, and language use.

The thesis, the organization of ideas, and the support make the framework of a good essay. Before the actual writing begins, a writer must create a mental outline by establishing a thesis, or main idea, and one or more specific supporting ideas (the number of ideas will depend on the length and content of the essay). Supporting ideas should not be overcomplicated; they are simply ideas that justify or explain the thesis. The writer must introduce and explain each supporting idea, and the resultant supporting paragraph should answer the *why?* or *who cares?* questions that the thesis may evoke.

Once the thesis and supporting ideas are identified, writers must determine the order in which the ideas will appear in the essay. A good introduction usually explains the thesis and briefly introduces the supporting ideas. Explanation of the supporting ideas should follow, with each idea in its own paragraph. The final paragraph, the conclusion, usually restates the thesis or summarizes the main ideas of the essay.

Adhering to this mental outline when the writing begins will help the writer organize and develop the essay. Using the Organization and Development scoring guides to evaluate practice essays will help to reinforce the process skills. The Word Choice and Sentence Formation scoring guides will help to strengthen language skills—the vital counterpart to essay organization and development.

Pronunciation Guide

a — track
ā — mate
ä — father
â — care
e — pet
ē — be
i — bit
ī — bite
o — job
ō — wrote
ô — port, horse, **fought**
ōō — proof
ŏŏ — book
u — pun
ū — **you**
û — purr
ə — about, system, supper, circus
îr — steer
ë — Fr. coeur
oi — toy

Word List

Lesson 1
arable
camaraderie
desiccate
equanimity
frangible
interminable
litany
lugubrious
moratorium
replete
truncate
ubiquitous
vernacular
wrenching
zealous

Lesson 2
brigand
carte blanche
contemptuous
cosmopolitan
donnybrook
incantation
interlocutor
metamorphosis
nomenclature
nonchalant
procrustean
rife
sophistry
stygian
vestige

Lesson 3
abstemious
archaic
atelier
axiom
dulcet
expurgate
iniquity
patronizing
pellucid
peremptory
perspicacious
scapegoat
talisman
usurp
vacillate

Lesson 4
apocryphal
catharsis
crepuscular
efficacious
estrange
internecine
intrinsic
inundate
kudos
maxim
putrid
revere
risible
servile
sybaritic

Lesson 5
anomaly
compendium
comprise
consternation
coterie
disconcert
eidetic
expiate
flippancy
foist
incongruous
innocuous
plethora
preamble
vitriolic

Lesson 6
accoutrement
antediluvian
contrive
haughty
hubris
imbroglio
peregrination
platitude
prognosticate
quotidian
sanctimonious
scullion
sectarian
stringent
venerate

Lesson 7	Lesson 9	Lesson 11
anecdote	benign	bulwark
churlish	blithe	canard
coeval	bumpkin	cortege
cogent	corroborate	crescendo
convoluted	culpable	demotic
dilatory	frenetic	disingenuous
entreat	hortatory	dogged
gibberish	indecorous	etymology
incumbent	orotund	impresario
inimical	penultimate	intransigent
livid	pervasive	malaise
lurid	provocative	requisite
nexus	recrimination	simian
promulgate	soporific	solecism
staid	toady	wont

Lesson 8	Lesson 10	Lesson 12
aleatory	circuitous	assiduous
allay	circumlocution	bellicose
ameliorate	depredate	compunction
asperity	indolent	condescending
exegesis	largesse	epiphany
inveigh	luminous	panacea
lionize	majordomo	physiognomy
otiose	perambulate	propensity
pander	perquisite	pulchritude
profligate	perquisite	revel
puerile	polemical	rhapsodize
recalcitrant	probity	sepulcher
renunciation	tacit	umbrage
unimpeachable	timorous	voluble
vitiate	untenable	wizened
	veneer	

<u>Lesson 13</u>
analgesic
conflagration
discretionary
draconian
florid
flummox
fractious
histrionics
implicate
moribund
noisome
punctilious
turpitude
unpalatable
veritable

<u>Lesson 14</u>
artisan
boondoggle
curmudgeon
fiduciary
inculcate
indiscernible
moiety
opprobrium
phlegmatic
potentate
protégé
reciprocate
repugnant
tenable
virulent

<u>Lesson 15</u>
appellation
autonomy
chthonian
coagulate
extirpate
gustatory
jurisprudence
malevolent
misanthrope
peripatetic
prominent
puissance
scion
supercilious
tutelary

<u>Lesson 16</u>
arcane
bourgeois
exculpate
indefeasible
matriculate
mercurial
nascent
paladin
salubrious
sine qua non
squelch
tangential
trenchant
tyro
vicissitude

<u>Lesson 17</u>
alimentary
ascetic
attenuate
attribute
celerity
congenital
depravity
discourse
encomium
ethereal
megalomania
mutable
primordial
remuneration
tactile

<u>Lesson 18</u>
cumulative
exhilaration
extricate
goad
impunity
lithe
poignant
propriety
pundit
satiate
superfluous
surfeit
trite
venial
vituperative

Lesson 19	Lesson 20	Lesson 21
abjure	acme	abrogate
dissipate	cerebral	analects
extant	conundrum	anomie
fulsome	deleterious	apostasy
inchoate	discerning	cognizant
inveterate	echelon	extrinsic
propitious	hypocrisy	factotum
rescind	idyllic	febrile
schism	malinger	magniloquent
spurious	nondescript	outré
stentorian	punitive	parity
transient	relegate	propinquity
tremulous	serendipity	prosaic
unwieldy	soluble	supine
utilitarian	waive	surreptitious

Lesson One

1. **camaraderie** (kä mə rä´ də rē) *n.* rapport and goodwill
    The coach attributed the team's success to the *camaraderie* among the players.
    syn: friendship; amity   *ant: enmity; hostility*

2. **frangible** (fran´ jə bəl) *adj.* fragile; easy to break
    Mom seldom removed the *frangible*, antique dishes from the cabinet.
    syn: delicate; breakable   *ant: sturdy; strong*

3. **litany** (li´ tə nē) *n.* a long, repetitive, or dull account
    The dissatisfied customer read a *litany* of complaints to the company representative.

4. **moratorium** (mor ə tōr´ ē əm) *n.* a suspension of activity; an authorized delay
    The warring factions declared a *moratorium* on combat during the peace talks.
    syn: cessation; postponement   *ant: rush; continuation*

5. **zealous** (zel´ əs) *adj.* fervent; fanatical
    The *zealous* gardener planted so many flowers that a number of them did not have the necessary space in which to grow.
    syn: passionate; enthusiastic   *ant: uninterested; indifferent*

6. **desiccate** (des´ i kāt) *v.* to dry out; to remove moisture
    Janet *desiccates* flowers and then uses them to make wreaths.
    syn: dehydrate   *ant: moisten; dampen*

7. **wrenching** (rench´ ing) *adj.* causing mental or physical pain
    The *wrenching* photographs of the starving children prompted Mike to send a donation.
    syn: distressing; agonizing   *ant: pleasant; comforting*

8. **replete** (ri plēt´) *adj.* full; abundant
    The anglers were happy to find their stream *replete* with trout.
    syn: abounding; rife   *ant: lacking; empty*

9. **interminable** (in tûr´ mə nə bəl) *adj.* tiresome and long; seemingly endless
The last few hours of school before the holiday vacation seemed *interminable*.
syn: tedious   *ant: fleeting; limited*

10. **arable** (ar´ ə bəl) *adj.* suitable for cultivation of land
Death Valley and the Badlands are both characterized by their lack of *arable* soil.
syn: fertile; fecund   *ant: barren; infertile*

11. **lugubrious** (lə gōō´ brē əs) *adj.* mournful; gloomy
The *lugubrious* funeral scene temporarily interrupted the comic tone of the play.
syn: somber; depressing   *ant: joyful*

12. **truncate** (trung´ kāt) *v.* to shorten
The candidate *truncated* his campaign because of a family illness.
syn: abridge; abbreviate   *ant: lengthen; increase*

13. **ubiquitous** (yōō bik´ wi təs) *adj.* occurring or seeming to occur everywhere; omnipresent
The camping trip was horrible; the mosquitoes were *ubiquitous* and hungry.
syn: universal   *ant: nonexistent*

14. **vernacular** (vər nak´ yə lər) *n.* everyday language
Using slang or *vernacular* in a formal term paper is usually inappropriate.

15. **equanimity** (ēk wə nim´ i tē) *n.* composure; calmness
Oddly enough, the plaintiff recounted the story of her attack with perfect *equanimity*.
syn: poise; sangfroid   *ant: anxiety; agitation*

Exercise I

Words in Context

From the list below, supply the words needed to complete the paragraph. Some words will not be used.

litany   truncate   lugubrious   camaraderie
equanimity   interminable   zealous

1. Tony brushed the rain off his jacket as he walked through the glass doors to
    the school. It was a[n] _____ Saturday morning, so Tony was happy
    that the assessment test was not scheduled for a beautiful spring day. He
    sat down with his answer booklet, and the test proctor began the standard,
    twenty-minute _____ of instructions, as though the _____,
    four-hour test were not long enough without the elaborate instructions.
    Tony, not at all nervous after having taken the test three times already,
    listened to the proctor with _____; however, some of the more
    _____ test-takers anxiously tapped their #2 pencils, eager to begin
    filling in the hundreds of tiny circles on their answer sheets.

From the list below, supply the words needed to complete the paragraph. Some words will not be used.

frangible   desiccated   arable   ubiquitous
replete   vernacular   zealous

2. Abby had taken Spanish in high school, but she had trouble understanding
    the shopkeeper's _____. The little shop was _____ with the
    things that tourists often needed, such as film, medicine, and long-distance
    phone cards; a shelf in front of the counter contained the hundreds of
    keychains, coffee mugs, old, _____ hard candies, and tee shirts
    _____ in every souvenir shop. A row of _____ vases and pottery
    on a shelf behind the counter caught Abby's eye, but she had actually come
    in to ask about the exotic plants growing in the _____ plot outside,
    behind the store.

From the list below, supply the words needed to complete the paragraph. Some words will not be used.

litany   truncate   camaraderie   wrenching
moratorium   arable   desiccate

3. After the _____ on racing during a storm had been lifted and the track dried, spectators watched the _____ and ease among members of the pit crews as they made adjustments to cars in the minutes before drivers could return to the track. Despite the excitement in the air, the whole scene was depressing for Miles, a former driver who had to watch the race from the stands. The eight titanium pins holding his leg bones together never let him forget the _____ injury that had _____ his once-promising racing career.

Exercise II

Sentence Completion

Complete the sentence in a way that shows you understand the meaning of the italicized vocabulary word.

1. When Angie complained about having to do chores for her allowance, her dad began his usual *litany* about…

2. It's difficult to maintain one's *equanimity* when…

3. The cooler at the picnic was *replete* with…

4. Dirk began to question the *camaraderie* of his teammates when one of them…

5. The actor became frustrated when the *ubiquitous* tabloid reporters…

6. Anita wanted a home with an *arable* yard where she could…

7. The *interminable* wait at the checkout line made Raymond decide…

8. When you pack the boxes for the move, put the *frangible* items…

9. Between innings, one of the *zealous* fans at the game…

10. Bill likes comic poems, but Sylvia prefers *lugubrious* ones that…

11. The NCAA imposed a brief *moratorium* on Central University's football games when several athletes...

12. Shelly used common *vernacular* to identify the animals, but the zoology professor wanted her to...

13. You will need to *truncate* your award speech if you find out...

14. Giles tried to suppress his *wrenching* memories of...

15. The pioneers *desiccated* some of the beef so that they...

Exercise III

Roots, Prefixes, and Suffixes

Study the entries and answer the questions that follow.

The prefix *ortho* means "straight" or "correct."
The prefix *hetero* means "different."
The prefix *homo* means "same."
The roots *dogm* and *dox* mean "belief."
The root *gen* means "type."
The suffix *logy* means "word."

1. *Using literal translations as guidance, define the following words without using a dictionary.*

   A. dogmatic
   B. heterodox
   C. homogenous
   D. orthodox
   E. doxology
   F. heterogeneous

2. If *para* means "beyond," then a *paradox* is something that is _____.

3. List as many words as you can think of that begin with the prefix *ortho*.

4. What is *homogenized* milk?

5. Give an example of a *dogma*.

6. List as many words as you can think of that contain the root *gen*.

Exercise IV

Inference

Complete the sentences by inferring information about the italicized word from its context.

1. That is a *ubiquitous* species of tree, so don't be surprised if, during your vacation abroad, you...

2. If you have *arable* ground on your property, then you might consider...

3. If you are bored, and the weather is *lugubrious*, you might...

Exercise V

Writing

Here is a writing prompt similar to the one you will find on the essay writing portion of the ACT.

Entertainment today, both in film and literature, is rife with misdirected judgments. When we read books or watch films set in historical contexts of the mid-1800s or earlier, we tend to weigh the behavior of characters against our expectations for people of the present. The featured heroes, or even the sympathetic characters, tend to be those who stand out among their contemporaries by espousing beliefs or attitudes of the present. This causes the other characters, representing the status quo, to seem primitive, or even barbaric, by comparison.

This often unconscious "judgment" that we render upon fiction is best described as *presentism*, an act of applying the values and beliefs of the present to the people—real or fictional—of past generations, cultures, and civilizations. There is a perpetual debate over the virtue of the founders of America, some of whom blazed frontiers, engaged in fierce battles, and established a successful republic, but were simultaneously practitioners of slavery or participants in campaigns against native Americans.

By present-day mores and beliefs, of course, slavery and genocide are regarded as abject evils, but does this make the successful figures of the past, and the fruits of their labor—the nation—evil? Should our predecessors be regarded as evil because they espoused corporal punishment, and profitted from child labor?

Take a position and explain whether or not the heroes of the past, or the people regarded as notable figures in history, should be celebrated for their achievements or forgotten due to their participation in societal norms that offend modern sensibilities. Imagine that your argument will become the preface to a collection of biographies of people know for their historical achievements in science, exploration, literature, or any other field.

Thesis: Write a *one-sentence* response to the above assignment. Make certain this single sentence offers a clear statement of your position.

Example: Because society's expectations, choices, and more were different in earlier times, people who lived then should not be judged by today's mores.

_____

_____

Organizational Plan: List at least three subtopics you will use to support your main idea. This list is your outline.

1. _____

2. _____

3. _____

Draft: Following your outline, write a good first draft of your essay. Remember to support all your points with examples, facts, references to reading, etc.

Review and revise: Exchange essays with a classmate. Using the scoring guide for Organization on page 240, score your partner's essay (while he or she scores yours). Focus on the organizational plan and use of language conventions. If necessary, rewrite your essay to improve the organizational plan and your use of language.

Exercise VI

English Practice

Identifying Sentence Errors
Identify the errors in the following sentences. Choose the answer that fixes the error.
If the sentence contains no error, select NO CHANGE.

1. Many individuals believe that if you are polite to their neighbors, you can be impolite to your families.
   A. NO CHANGE
   B. Many individuals believe that if they are polite to their neighbors, they can be impolite to their families.
   C. Many people believe that if people are polite to their neighbors, it is fine to be impolite to their families.
   D. Many people believe that if they are polite to their neighbors, it is fine to be impolite to their own families.

2. The commonly known expression that "a dog is a man's best friend" is frequently incorrect; all a person has to do is read the newspaper.
   F. NO CHANGE
   G. that "a dog is mans' best friend"
   H. which "dog is man's best friend"
   J. that a dog is a man's best friend

3. The home run Hal hit flew out of the stadium sailed into the parking lot, and smashed the window of a brand-new car.
   A. NO CHANGE
   B. stadium: sailed into the parking lot,
   C. stadium, sailed into the parking lot,
   D. stadium, and into the parking lot,

4. Until one of the members of the rival gangs propose a truce, there will be no safety for honest citizens of this city.
   F. NO CHANGE
   G. member of the rival gangs proposes
   H. members of the rival gang propose
   J. members of the rival gangs proposes

5. No matter how hard Theresa tries, she cannot win the approval of her field hockey coach.
   A. NO CHANGE
   B. approval for
   C. approval to
   D. approval from

Improving Sentences

The underlined portion of each sentence below contains some flaw. Select the answer that best corrects the flaw.

6. Scientists think of the underwater world beneath the sea as a vast laboratory, in which strange creatures do odd, unexplained things.
   - F. Scientists believe the underwater world beneath the sea is a vast laboratory
   - G. Scientists feel that the underwater world beneath the sea is a vast laboratory
   - H. Scientists think the underwater world is a vast laboratory
   - J. A vast laboratory is how scientists view the underwater world beneath the sea

7. Ben Franklin was a statesman, politician, printer, author, philosopher, inventor, and Ambassador to France, yet most people studying history in school only think of him as a man standing in a lightning storm with a kite and a key.
   - A. yet only most people that study history in school think of him as a man standing in a lightning storm with a kite and a key.
   - B. yet most people with only a tiny knowledge of high school history think of him as a man standing in a lightning storm with a kite and a key.
   - C. yet most people who don't know much history only think of him as a man standing in a lightning storm with a kite and a key.
   - D. yet most students think of him only as a man standing in a storm with a kite and a key.

8. "The reason I choose not to," said the potential customer to the car salesman, "is because of the fact that you have not given me enough for my trade-in."
   - F. "Is because of the fact that you have not given me enough for my trade-in."
   - G. "is because of you having not given me enough for my trade-in."
   - H. "is because you have not given me enough for my trade-in."
   - J. "is that you have not given me enough for my trade-in."

9. There is only one prerequisite for the <u>job; You must have a college degree</u>
    <u>in Physics.</u>
    A. job: you must have a college degree in physics.
    B. job; you must have a college degree in Physics.
    C. job. That is that you must have a college degree in Physics.
    D. job, and it is that a college degree in physics is necessary.

10. <u>Ever since he has devoted himself entirely to helping the homeless.</u>
    F. Ever since he devoted himself entirely to helping the homeless.
    G. Ever since, he has devoted himself entirely to helping the homeless.
    H. Ever since he has entirely devoted himself to helping the homeless.
    J. Ever since helping the homeless, he has devoted himself entirely to it.

Vocabulary
Power Plus
for the
ACT
Vocabulary,
Reading, and Writing
Exercises for High Scores

Lesson Two

1.   **metamorphosis** (met ə môr´ fə sis)   *n.*   a transformation or dramatic change
     That butterfly will experience a physical *metamorphosis* as it passes from the pupa stage to the adult stage.
     syn: mutation   *ant: stasis*

2.   **donnybrook** (don´ ē brŏŏk)   *n.*   a fight; an uproar
     During the last minute of the close championship game, a referee's foolish decision caused a *donnybrook* among the fans of both teams.
     syn: brawl; quarrel; altercation   *ant: agreement*

3.   **nonchalant** (non shə länt´)   *adj.*   unconcerned; indifferent
     The *nonchalant* banker looked at the million-dollar check as though he saw one every day.
     syn: detached; relaxed   *ant: excited; concerned; alarmed*

4.   **vestige** (ves´ tij)   *n.*   a trace or evidence of something that once existed
     The rich vein of coal is a *vestige* of Earth's lush, prehistoric forests.
     syn: remnant; hint

5.   **interlocutor** (in tər lok´ yə tər)   *n.*   someone who participates in a conversation
     The delusional man wandered down the street, conversing with some invisible *interlocutor.*

6.   **procrustean** (prō krəs´ tē ən)   *adj.*   strictly disregarding individual differences or circumstances
     The *procrustean* teacher warned the class that he would accept no excuses for tardiness.
     syn: ruthless; undiscriminating   *ant: sympathetic; compassionate*

7.   **stygian** (sti´ jē ən)   *adj.*   dark and forbidding
     The *stygian* house, empty for decades, was often the source of unexplained phenomena.
     syn: shadowy   *ant: bright; illuminated*

8. **sophistry** (sä´ fə strē) *n.* a deliberately deceptive or misleading argument
    The TV talk-show host's convincing *sophistry* made his guests look foolish for disagreeing with him.
    syn: chicanery; ruse   *ant: truth*

9. **carte blanche** (kärt blänch´) *n.* boundless authority; unlimited power to act
    The secret agent had *carte blanche* to complete the extremely vital mission.
    syn: license; sanction; free rein   *ant: restriction*

10. **incantation** (in kan tā´ shən) *n.* a chant; a recited magical spell
    The sorceress uttered a long *incantation* as she mixed the magic potion.
    syn: invocation

11. **cosmopolitan** (koz mə pol´ i tn) *adj.* worldly; sophisticated
    Brett longed to have the *cosmopolitan* lifestyle of an international investor.
    syn: cultured   *ant: provincial*

12. **rife** (rīf) *adj.* abundant; prevalent
    Be careful while shopping, because that part of the city is *rife* with crime.
    syn: overflowing; rampant   *ant: lacking; limited*

13. **nomenclature** (nō´ mən klā chər) *n.* technical names or naming system in an art or science
    Students often spend hours memorizing the *nomenclature* of organic chemistry.
    syn: terminology

14. **brigand** (brig´ ənd) *n.* a robber or bandit
    The stagecoach driver kept a nervous watch for *brigands* while transporting the heavy cash box.
    syn: highwayman; outlaw

15. **contemptuous** (kən temp´ chŏŏ əs) *adj.* haughty; scornful
    The *contemptuous* bank loan officer was rude to the poorly dressed applicants.
    syn: arrogant; derisive   *ant: humble; polite*

Exercise I

Words in Context

From the list below, supply the words needed to complete the paragraph. Some words will not be used.

donnybrook	cosmopolitan	carte blanche	vestige
procrustean	incantation	metamorphosis	

1. Mr. Trunk, the new manager, walked into his new, albeit antiquated, office. The only _____ of the former manager was a dusty hotrod calendar, three years out of date. Recruited for his _____ leadership style and general lack of compassion, Mr. Trunk promised the company president that production would experience a[n] _____ for the better before the end of the year. Trunk had _____ to change operations any way he saw fit, though he knew that his changes would not be taken lightly; his revisions of break and lunchtime policies nearly got him into a[n] _____ with angry workers, who felt that they had been wronged.

From the list below, supply the words needed to complete the paragraph. Some words will not be used.

rife	nonchalant	donnybrook	interlocutor
contemptuous	nomenclature	brigand	

2. The _____ sprang from the hedges, produced his saber, and ordered the obviously wealthy couple to surrender their valuables, but the couple's _____ reaction to the threat bewildered the thief.

    "How _____ you aristocrats are," said the robber. "An outlaw threatens your lives, and you just stare with indifference?"

    "Yes, because they have nothing to fear. Lower your weapon, highwayman." The sudden voice of a new _____ startled the thief, but not as much as the sharp tip of the dagger jabbing into his shoulder blade. The thief dropped his sword, regreting he had not seen the watchman approaching from behind. To reduce the serious crime that had become _____ in the district, government king had recruited extra officers to patrol the cobblestone streets.

From the list below, supply the words needed to complete the paragraph. Some words will not be used.

stygian   brigand   incantation   cosmopolitan
carte blanche nomenclature   sophistry

3.   In an effort to overcome the overwhelming boredom of his _____, stone-floored prison cell, Tobias exercised his knowledge by identifying each insect he saw by its Latin _____. The only alternative he had was to listen to the prisoner in the neighboring cell shout the same _____ that had failed to convince the judge that he was innocent. In several weeks, the repetitive, daily rant began to sound like a[n] _____ to Tobias, perhaps a spell that would melt the bars of the noisy prisoner's cell. The two prisoners conversed occasionally. Tobias, a well-traveled, renowned explorer, related tales from his _____ life, but the conversation inevitably returned to the topic of the other man's wrongful imprisonment.

Exercise II

Sentence Completion

Complete the sentence in a way that shows you understand the meaning of the italicized vocabulary word.

1.   The *brigands* plotted to rob the train by…

2.   Paul experienced a total *metamorphosis* in his behavior after…

3.   The *contemptuous* child wondered why none of his classmates…

4.   A *donnybrook* erupted at the grocery store when…

5.   Most people know that H_2O is the chemical *nomenclature* for…

6.   The fans in the home crowd yelled a hilarious *incantation* when…

7.   The *procrustean* bus driver refused to…

8.   The *stygian* cave made a good hideout for the outlaw because…

9.   Kelly thought herself too *cosmopolitan* to…

10. The lawn is *rife* with weeds this year because…

11. The cement foundation, overgrown with weeds, and littered with charred wood, is the only remaining *vestige* of...

12. George was a great *interlocutor* in the debate because he...

13. Ian had *carte blanche* when using the family car until he...

14. Try to remain *nonchalant* and avoid looking desperate when we ask...

15. The arch villain used *sophistry* to convince the hero to...

Exercise III

Roots, Prefixes, and Suffixes

Study the entries and answer the questions that follow.

The suffix *escent* means "becoming" or "growing."
The prefix *ob* means "toward" or "against."
The prefix *con* means "totally" or "completely."
The root *val* means "strong" or "healthy."
The root *rub* means "red."
The roots *irid* and *iris* mean "rainbow" or "brightly colored."
The root *fac* means "make."

1. Using literal translations as guidance, define the following words without using a dictionary.

   A. rubefacient   D. convalescent
   B. iridescent   E. iris
   C. rubescent   F. valor

2. What do you think the musical term *crescendo* means?

3. List some of the deeds that a *valiant* knight might do.

4. List as many words as you can think of that contain the root *val*.

Exercise IV

Inference

Complete the sentences by inferring information about the italicized word from its context.

1. The forest around the house is *rife* with poison ivy, so we should...

2. Mike used to be rebellious, but he experienced a *metamorphosis* that...

3. If Nina behaved in a *nonchalant* manner when she saw her report card, then she probably...

Exercise V

Critical Reading

Below is a reading passage followed by several multiple-choice questions similar to the ones you will encounter on the ACT. Carefully read the passage and choose the best answer for each of the questions.

Edward Sanford Martin (1856-1939) was a humor writer and one of the founders of Life Magazine. The following passage is an excerpt from Martin's essay, "The Tyranny of Things." In the essay, Martin discusses how easily people become slaves to material goods, including even material things that are thought to be beneficial or coveted, such as large homes.

There was a story in the newspapers the other day about a Massachusetts minister who resigned his charge because someone had given his parish a fine house, and his parishioners wanted him to live in it. His salary was too small, he said, to admit of his living in a big house, and he would not do it. He was even
5 deaf to the proposal that he should share the proposed tenement with the sewing societies and clubs of his church, and when the matter came to a serious issue, he relinquished his charge and sought a new field of usefulness. The situation was an amusing instance of the embarrassment of riches. Let no one to whom restricted quarters may have grown irksome, and who covets larger dimensions of shelter, be
10 too hasty in deciding that the minister was wrong. Did you ever see the house that Hawthorne lived in at Lenox? Did you ever see Emerson's house at Concord? They are good houses for Americans to know and remember. They permitted thought.

A big house is one of the greediest cormorants which can light upon a little income. Backs may go threadbare and stomachs may worry along on indifferent
15 filling, but a house *will* have things, though its occupants go without. It is rarely complete, and constantly tempts the imagination to flights in brick and dreams in lath and plaster. It develops annual thirsts for paint and wallpaper, at least, if not for marble and woodcarving. The plumbing in it must be kept in order on pain of death. Whatever price is put on coal, it has to be heated in winter; and if it is rural
20 or suburban, the grass about it must be cut even though funerals in the family have to be put off for the mowing. If the tenants are not rich enough to hire p-eople to keep their house clean, they must do it themselves, for there is no excuse that will pass among housekeepers for a dirty house. The master of a house too big for him may expect to spend the leisure which might be made intellectually or spiritually
25 profitable, in acquiring and putting into practice fag ends of the arts of the plumber, the bell-hanger, the locksmith, the gas-fitter, and the carpenter. Presently he will know how to do everything that can be done in the house, except enjoy himself. He will learn about taxes, too, and water-rates, and how such abominations as sewers or new pavements are always liable to accrue at his expense. As for the mistress,
30 she will be a slave to carpets and curtains, wallpaper, painters, and women who come in by the day to clean. She will be lucky if she gets a chance to say her prayers, and thrice and four times happy when she can read a book or visit with her friends. To live in a big house may be a luxury, provided that one has a full set of money and an enthusiastic housekeeper in one's family; but to scrimp in a big
35 house is a miserable business. Yet such is human folly, that for a man to refuse to live in a house because it is too big for him, is such an exceptional exhibition of sense that it becomes the favorite paragraph of a day in the newspapers.

An ideal of earthly comfort, so common that every reader must have seen it, is to get a house so big that it is burdensome to maintain, and fill it up so full of
40 gimcracks that it is a constant occupation to keep it in order. Then, when the expense of living in it is so great that you can't afford to go away and rest from the burden of it, the situation is complete and boarding houses and cemeteries begin to yawn for you. How many Americans, do you suppose, out of the droves that flock annually to Europe, are running away from oppressive houses?

45 When nature undertakes to provide a house, it fits the occupant. Animals which build by instinct build only what they need, but man's building instinct, if it gets a chance to spread itself at all, is boundless, just as all his instincts are. For it is man's peculiarity that nature has filled him with impulses to do things, and left it to his discretion when to stop. She never tells him when he has finished. And
50 perhaps we ought not to be surprised that in so many cases it happens that he does not know, but just goes ahead as long as the materials last.

If another *man* tries to oppress him, he understands that and is ready to fight to death and sacrifice all he has, rather than submit; but the tyranny of things is so subtle, so gradual in its approach, and comes so masked with seeming benefits, that
55 it has him hopelessly bound before he suspects his fetters. He says from day to day, "I will add thus to my house;" "I will have one or two more horses;" "I will make a little greenhouse in my garden;" "I will allow myself the luxury of another hired man;" and so he goes on having things and imagining that he is richer for them.

Presently he begins to realize that it is the things that own him. He has piled them
60 up on his shoulders, and there they sit like Sinbad's Old Man and drive him; and
it becomes a daily question whether he can keep his trembling legs or not.

All of which is not meant to prove that property has no real value, or to rebut
Charles Lamb's scornful denial that enough is as good as a feast. It is not meant to
apply to the rich, who can have things comfortably, if they are philosophical; but
65 to us poor, who have constant need to remind ourselves that where the verbs to
have and to be cannot both be completely inflected, the verb to be is the one that
best repays concentration.

1.   The tone of this passage is best described as
    A. cynical.
    B. supportive.
    C. forlorn.
    D. evasive.

2.   As used in the first paragraph, *charge* most nearly means
    F. accusation.
    G. debt.
    H. ridicule.
    J. duty.

3.   According to the context of the first paragraph, Emerson's and
    Hawthorne's houses were probably
    A. elaborate and expansive.
    B. practical, plain residences.
    C. larger than the homes of their neighbors.
    D. simple tents with dirt floors.

4.   The *cormorants* in line 13 are probably
    F. strike-anywhere matches.
    G. feelings of doubt.
    H. bands of robbers.
    J. voracious sea birds.

5. Which choice is the best interpretation of the following quotation?

    "Backs may go threadbare and stomachs may worry along on indifferent filling, but a house *will* have things, though its occupants go without."

    A. The maintenance of a house always takes priority over the people living in it, even if they are forced to go without proper food or clothing.
    B. It's a bad time to buy real estate because interest rates are rising and the price of food and clothing is increasing.
    C. No matter how much money someone has, a house will ensure that he or she will not be able to afford to eat or buy clothing.
    D. People inevitably spend too much money on their homes.

6. According to paragraph 2, there is nothing wrong with living in a large house if
    F. the house contains no decorations or furniture.
    G. the occupants are familiar with tax laws, painting, and mowing grass.
    H. the occupants have plenty of money and someone to maintain the house.
    J. the occupants have no friends who do not pay rent or refuse to help with repairs.

7. As used in line 34, *scrimp* most nearly means
    A. to live.
    B. to economize.
    C. to repair.
    D. to spend freely.

8. According to the author, people such as the minister are accused of having an "embarrassment of riches" because
    F. few people understand why someone would refuse to live in a large house.
    G. the house offered to the minister is bedecked with fine woodwork.
    H. everyone wants a larger house than the one he or she currently owns.
    J. a modest, wealthy person would never accept a free house.

9. Which choice best paraphrases the following quotation?

    "but to us poor, who have constant need to remind ourselves that
    where the verbs *to have* and *to be* cannot both be completely inflected,
    the verb *to be* is the one that best repays concentration."

    A. Those who cannot be happy simply existing, or "being," become
       disillusioned by "wanting" all the time.
    B. The poor, who need more than they want, are usually happier to
       think about what kind of people they are.
    C. The poor, who cannot claim to have or have had material things, are
       better off considering "what they are" than "what they have."
    D. Wealthy people, who know who they are and what they want, have
       little need to worry about owning a large house.

10. Which of the following statements best supports the theme of this passage?
    F. Large houses require a lot of work.
    G. A free house, small or large, is always better than no house.
    H. People become slaves to their material possessions.
    J. Large families should reconsider whether they require large homes.

Vocabulary
Power Plus
for the
ACT
Vocabulary,
Reading, and Writing
Exercises for High Scores

Lesson Three

1. **scapegoat** (skāp´ gōt) *n.* one who bears the blame for others
    Andy was frequently absent, so other workers made him the *scapegoat* for their own mistakes.
    syn: patsy; sucker

2. **peremptory** (pə remp´ tə rē) *adj.* not allowing refusal or delay; imperative
    The guard issued a *peremptory* warning to step away from the fence or be fired upon.
    syn: authoritative; unconditional   *ant: roundabout; passive; equivocal*

3. **atelier** (a təl yā´) *n.* an artist's or a designer's workshop
    The painter converted his garage into an *atelier* to work on his creative masterpieces.

4. **axiom** (ak´ sē əm) *n.* a universal truth; an established rule
    According to some people, the most important *axiom* of all is, "Do unto others as you would have them do unto you."
    syn: fundamental; theorem   *ant: absurdity*

5. **dulcet** (dul´ sit) *adj.* melodious; pleasing to the ear
    The opera singer's *dulcet* voice earned her a prominent place in the upcoming production.
    syn: harmonic; melodic   *ant: cacophonous; dissonant*

6. **usurp** (yōō sûrp´) *v.* to take over; to seize power
    The plotting general planned to *usurp* power while the elderly ruler was ill.
    syn: commandeer; seize; co-opt   *ant: abdicate; relinquish*

7. **patronizing** (pā´ trə nīz ing) *adj.* treating with condescension; acting superior
    Despite his *patronizing* treatment of the employees, the foreman was still well liked.
    syn: lofty; arrogant   *ant: humble; friendly*

8. **iniquity** (i nik´ wi tē) *n.* an evil or wicked act
    He heartily repented his *iniquities,* but only after he faced a lifelong prison sentence.
    syn: abomination; injustice; sin

9. **archaic** (är kā´ ik) *adj.* no longer current or applicable; antiquated
   Some states still have *archaic* laws that regulate horse-and-buggy traffic.
   syn: obsolete; outmoded   *ant: current; modern*

10. **vacillate** (vas´ ə lāt) *v.* to waver; to sway indecisively
    For years Bobby *vacillated* between liking one band and then another.
    syn: fluctuate; swing; waffle   *ant: decide*

11. **perspicacious** (pûr spi kā´ shəs) *adj.* keen; mentally sharp
    The *perspicacious* gambler knew that he would need to make a hasty exit
    after winning most of the cowboys' money.
    syn: shrewd; keen; clever   *ant: dull; stupid*

12. **abstemious** (ab stē´ mē əs) *adj.* using or consuming sparingly
    Bill, who wants to lose weight, is *abstemious* in eating foods high in fat.
    syn: frugal; moderate   *ant: gluttonous; greedy*

13. **talisman** (tal´ is mən) *n.* a magic charm or superstitious object for
          protection or luck
    The wizard claimed that no harm would come to anyone holding the
    talisman.

14. **expurgate** (ek´ spər gāt) *v.* to remove vulgar or objectionable material
    Censors sometimes feel that it is necessary to *expurgate* offensive
    scenes from movies.
    syn: censor; bowdlerize; sanitize

15. **pellucid** (pə lōō´ sid) *adj.* transparent; clear
    Eliminate extraneous words if you want your paper to have a *pellucid*
    message.
    syn: limpid   *ant: obscure; opaque*

Exercise I

Words in Context

From the list below, supply the words needed to complete the paragraph. Some words will not be used.

usurp	atelier	pellucid	archaic
axiom	dulcet	iniquity	

1. "I prefer to think of this factory as a giant _atelier_, where a team of artists creates not specialized tools, but hand-machined works of art," said Roger, the owner of Calumette Industries. "And as long as our goal remains _pellucid_ to every employee, this company will soar." Roger, who took over the failing operation just months ago, sparked life back into the floundering plant by replacing _archaic_ industry practices with new methods guaranteed to increase production; however, despite Roger's many changes to the plant, he was quick to note that he is a firm believer in the _axiom_, "Don't fix things that aren't broken."
    During a tour of the factory one could see by the smile on Roger's face that the repetitive clanging of electric motors and hydraulic presses was _dulcet_ music to the industrialist's ears.

From the list below, supply the words needed to complete the paragraph. Some words will not be used.

scapegoat	atelier	iniquity	vacillated
perspicacious	expurgate	talisman	

2. When an obscene photograph appeared in the school yearbook, the administration immediately sought a[n] _scapegoat_ to take the blame for what the community called "a[n] _iniquity_." Angry students and parents blamed Dora, the yearbook editor, for not being _perspicacious_ enough to have spotted the photo before the book was sent to the printer. The school collected the books and returned them to the printer to _expurgate_ the photograph. Dora, a junior, _vacillated_ over whether she would sign up for the yearbook staff again next year.

From the list below, supply the words needed to complete the paragraph. Some words will not be used.

talisman   archaic   abstemious   scapegoat
patronizing   usurp   peremptory

3.   Paranoid that someone would _____ control of his latest project, Bob carried the scale model of the building with him all around the office as though it were some kind of _____ that would protect him from any dragons hiding in the cubicles. Some of the employees giggled when Bob walked by, and others gave him _____ looks, which made him feel like a fearful toddler carrying a security blanket. Mrs. Simmons, the manager, began to worry that perhaps Bob was stressed out, so she called a meeting with him. During the meeting, the manager reminded Bob that his _____ use of vacation time was not healthy; he absolutely must get away from the office for a little while. Two weeks later, as Bob basked in the Caribbean sun, he wished that the boss would have prescribed this kind of _____ vacation months earlier.

Exercise II

Sentence Completion

Complete the sentence in a way that shows you understand the meaning of the italicized vocabulary word.

1. Chris knew that he would become the *scapegoat* if the police learned that he...

2. Uncle Pete thought that carrying a *talisman*, such as a rabbit's foot, would...
    bring him good luck

3. Catherine feared that someone would try to *usurp* her position at the company if she...

4. Virgil got lost in the city because his *archaic* map did not...

5. The gymnasium was once open to the public, but owing to the *iniquities* of a few vandals, it is now...

6. To ensure that Adam had a *pellucid* idea of what she was explaining, Sheila...

7. During the bomb scare, the principal issued a *peremptory* order to...

8. The *patronizing* babysitter told the children...

9. Occasionally, Lisa strayed from her *abstemious* budget in order to...

10. In his *atelier*, the carpenter...

11. At the store, Susan *vacillated* over which...

12. To *expurgate* the graffiti sprayed on the walls of the tunnel, the cleanup crew...

13. The fugitive would have escaped if a *perspicacious* citizen had not noticed...

14. While camping, Liz quickly fell asleep to the *dulcet* sound of...

15. Jerry often muttered the *axiom*, "If you want something done right, do it yourself," when...

Exercise III

Roots, Prefixes, and Suffixes

Study the entries and answer the questions that follow.

The root *ratio* means "reason."
The root *ment* means "mind."
The root *gno* means "knowledge."
The prefix *de* means "away."
The prefix *ir* means "not."
The prefix *a* means "without."
The prefix *pro* means "before" or "in advance."

1. Using literal translations as guidance, define the following words without
   using a dictionary.

   A. prognosticate   D. mentality
   B. agnostic   E. rationale
   C. irrational   F. dementia

2. Explain the difference between a *ratio* and a *ration*.

3. What do you think a *mentalist* does?

4. If *dia* means "through," or "by way of," what does the word *diagnosis*
   mean literally?

5. List as many words as you can think of that contain the root *ratio*.

Exercise IV

Inference

*Complete the sentences by inferring information about the italicized word from its
context.*

1. During the drought, the mayor asked citizens to be *abstemious* in their
   water consumption because...

2. If an *archaic* computer system will not run the latest software, the user will
   need to...

3. The answer to the calculus problem was not yet *pellucid* to Jack, so he...

Exercise V

Writing

Here is a writing prompt similar to the one you will find on the essay writing portion of the ACT.

Realism in the horror genre of cinema, in the early days of slasher films and monster movies, is almost a joke; cinema technology at the time of the rise of horror films was so primitive that gory scenes replete with food-based "blood" and cheap makeup "wounds" seemed as real to audiences as cartoons did. Modern special effects through computer-generated imagery (CGI), however, have rendered gore all too real, allowing audiences to experience—visually, at least—realistic scenes of depravity and violence unknown to anyone but victims of horrible crimes or disasters or denizens of combat zones, where death and horrid scenes of suffering are forced upon everyone. Many of the witnesses to such atrocities spend their lifetimes trying to forget the scenes that haunt their minds and slowly poison their spirits.

Obviously, watching horror scenes does not turn people into psychopaths, but does it have a negative effect? Can films, video games, or even grotesque literary imagery desensitize people to real horror and make them less responsive to the suffering of others, or is it possible to become more sympathetic toward victims by watching scenes of human misery?

Write a letter to the survivors of a brutal dictator's political prison who have been given refuge in the United States. Explain the role of horror fiction in our culture, and your opinion of the films and their entertainment value.

Thesis: Write a one-sentence response to the above assignment. Make certain this sentence offers a clear statement of your position.

Example: Because we enjoy, on average, a high quality of life, our culture is greatly distorted by prevalent images of death.

_____

_____

Organizational Plan: If your thesis is the point on which you want to end, where does your essay need to begin? List the points of development that are inevitable in leading your reader from your beginning point to your end point. This list is your outline.

1. _____

2. _____

3. _____

Draft: Use your thesis as both your beginning and your end. Following your outline, write a good first draft of your essay. Remember to support all of your points with examples, facts, references to reading, etc.

Review and revise: Exchange essays with a classmate. Using the scoring guide for Development on page 241, score your partner's essay (while he or she scores yours). Focus on the development of ideas and use of language conventions. If necessary, rewrite your essay to improve the development of ideas and/or your use of language.

Exercise VI

English Practice

Improving Paragraphs

Read the following passage and then choose the best revision for the underlined portions of the paragraph. The questions will require you to make decisions regarding the revision of the reading selection. Some revisions are not actual mistakes, but will improve the clarity of the writing.

[1]

(1) The world as we know it would not exist today if it were not for gigantic aircraft capable of carrying <u>hundreds of tons of people</u>,[1] supplies, and equipment. (2) The credit for inspiring such aircraft must go to a versatile Texan by the name of Howard Hughes—the inventor of the first massive "flying boat" that most now remember as the "Spruce Goose."

   1. A. NO CHANGE
      B. hundred's of tons of people
      C. hundreds of ton's of people
      D. many hundred tons of
        passengers

[2]

(3) Howard Hughes was what most would describe as a Renaissance man. (4) He was an actor, a director, a theater owner, a pilot, and an engineer. (5) Though he never finished high school, Hughes attended classes at California Institute of Technology, thanks to a considerable donation by his father. (6) Hughes's father was wealthy. (7) Hughes's father died when Hughes was only eighteen years old. (8) A judge awarded Hughes legal adulthood just after his nineteenth birthday, <u>that allowed</u>[2] the young man to take control of his father's estate from his uncle. (9) Part of the estate included Hughes Tool Company, and Hughes, taking advantage of the booming aircraft technology industry of the early twentieth century, formed the Hughes Aircraft Company division in 1932. (10) With this company and the help of famous shipbuilder Henry Kaiser, <u>they</u>[3] established a contract with the government to build three "flying boats." (11) Hughes never finished building three planes, but he did successfully complete one.

2. F. NO CHANGE	3. A. NO CHANGE
G. which allows	B. Kaiser and Hughes
H. that allows	C. Hughes
J. which allowed	D. the pair

4. Which sentence can be deleted
from paragraph 2 without
changing the intent of the
paragraph?
   F. sentence 3
   G. sentence 4
   H. sentence 6
   J. sentence 7

[3]

(12) To meet government specifications, Hughes's flying boat had to be capable of transporting cargo and men over long distances. (13) <u>Enemies' were</u>[5] destroying shipping lanes during World War II, and the military needed the flying boat to carry soldiers and supplies high above enemy ships and submarines. (14) The contract awarded Hughes <u>$18 million dollars</u>[6] to build the three aircraft, and Hughes added another seven million of his own fortune to fund the project. (15) With adequate funding and sheer determination, Hughes then proves to the world that human ingenuity could make a 200-ton pile of wood airborne.

5. A. NO CHANGE
   B. Enemys were
   C. Enemies was
   D. Enemies were

6. F. NO CHANGE
   G. eighteen million dollars
   H. 18 million dollars
   J. $18,000,000 million

7. Which of the following corrects an error in sentence 15?
   A. Specify which type of engineering requires ingenuity.
   B. Rewrite the sentence to omit the comma splice.
   C. Ingenuity is plural and requires a plural verb.
   D. Change "proves" to "proved."

[4]

(16) The public nicknamed the flying boat the "Spruce Goose" to mock Hughes for his apparent failure. (17) The flying boat was constructed of mostly birch wood (not spruce) and fabric. (18) It had a single hull, eight of the most powerful engines of the time, and a single vertical tail. (19) Hughes covered the primary control surfaces <u>in fabric and,</u>[8] the rest of the plane was laminated birch. (20) The plane was a behemoth—the largest aircraft built in the era—with a 320-foot wingspan, <u>219 feet in length,</u>[9] and a wing area of 11,430 square feet. (21) Most impressively, the flying boat could take off with a weight of 400,000 pounds, or 200 tons.

8 F. NO CHANGE
    G. fabric--and
    H. fabric, and
    J. fabric, and,

9. A. NO CHANGE
    B. 219 feet long,
    C. a length of 219 feet,
    D. 219 foot length,

[5]

(22) Though the giant plane flew, it flew only once. (23) On November 2, 1947, well after the end of the war and in the midst of Congressional hearings to determine why the planes were not yet completed, Hughes returned to California to run supposed engine tests on his plane. (24) In the waters off Long Beach, Hughes took the controls, shoved the throttles to the stops, and, to the amazement of onlookers, the Spruce Goose took flight. (25) Hughes lifted the plane 70 feet from the ocean and it lumbered along at 80 miles per hour for about a mile before making a perfect landing. (26) Many historians claim that while Congress decided to cancel the contract for the H-4 Hercules, the short flight of the mammoth plane vindicated Howard Hughes. (27) The flying boat may have been late, but it was well ahead of its <u>time to this day,</u>[10] the Spruce Goose is, by wingspan, the largest plane ever built. (28) After the historic flight was made by Hughes, the plane was moved to <u>it's hangar</u>[11] and was stored and maintained as though active until 1980, four years after the death of Howard Hughes. (29) It now rests in Oregon as a colossal artifact at the Evergreen Aviation Museum. (30) Someday, perhaps, Hughes's invention will inspire a new generation of inventors to do what others say cannot be done.

10.F. NO CHANGE
    G. time, to this day,
    H. time; to this day,
    J. time, to this day:

11.A. NO CHANGE
    B. its' hangar
    C. its hangar
    D. its, hangar

12.Which sentence from paragraph 4 should be moved to paragraph 5?
    F. sentence 16
    G. sentence 17
    H. sentence 18
    J. sentence 19

13.Which revision would best clarify the term "H-4 Hercules" in sentence 26?
    A. Replace all references to Hughes's plane with H-4 Hercules.
    B. Mention the official name of the Spruce Goose earlier in the passage.
    C. Explain why the plane is named after a mythical person.
    D. Replace H-4 Hercules with Flying Boat.

14. At which point in paragraph 5 should a new paragraph begin?
   F. between sentence 23 and 24
   G. between sentence 25 and 26
   H. between sentence 26 and 27
   J. between sentence 27 and 28

15. Which of the following suggestions would best improve sentence 28?
   A. Divide it into two separate sentences.
   B. Delete "four years after the death of Howard Hughes."
   C. Change the sentence from the passive voice to the active voice.
   D. Delete "and was stored."

Vocabulary
Power Plus
for the
ACT
Vocabulary,
Reading, and Writing
Exercises for High Scores

Lesson Four

1. **efficacious** (ef i kā´ shəs) *adj.* effective; producing the desired outcome
    The shot of adrenaline was *efficacious* in restarting the victim's heart.
    syn: productive; useful   *ant: ineffective*

2. **catharsis** (kə thär´ sis) *n.* a release of emotional tension
    The movie lacked a *catharsis* because the villain received no punishment.
    syn: purgation

3. **inundate** (in´ un dāt) *v.* to overwhelm; to fill beyond capacity
    Callers *inundated* the radio station with requests for the popular new song.
    syn: flood; overwhelm

4. **revere** (ri vîr´) *v.* to regard with respect, awe, or adoration
    Alexander the Great's soldiers *revered* their leader because he led the troops into every battle.
    syn: venerate; respect; honor   *ant: revile*

5. **internecine** (in tər ne´ sēn) *adj.* mutually destructive
    The *internecine* battle resulted in thousands of casualties, but neither side gained new land.
    ant: constructive; beneficial

6. **risible** (ri´ zə bəl) *adj.* relating to laughter; laughable
    The *risible* statement made by the gentleman in the front row was completely ridiculous, but it was amusing.
    syn: comical; jocular; jocund   *ant: grave; solemn*

7. **sybaritic** (si bə rit´ ik) *adj.* marked by luxury or pleasure
    Ice sculptures, massive chandeliers, and live entertainment were commonplace at Loren's *sybaritic* parties.
    syn: luxurious; ostentatious; grandiose   *ant: modest; simple; plain*

8. **crepuscular** (kri pus´ kyə lər) *adj.* pertaining to twilight
    That species of trout has *crepuscular* feeding habits, so you'll catch the most at daybreak or sunset.

9. **kudos**ˑ (kōō´ dōz) *n.* acclaim or praise
   The director of the successful new musical won *kudos* from most critics.
   syn: honor; distinction   *ant: disapproval; rejection*
   ˑ*Kudos is considered singular, not plural*

10. **estrange** (i stränj´) *v.* to alienate
    Jill's overbearing mother-in-law *estranged* Jill from her husband.
    syn: disaffect; antagonize   *ant: unite; endear*

11. **intrinsic** (in trin´ sik) *adj.* of or relating to a thing's basic nature;
    inherent
    Humans have an *intrinsic* desire to be loved.
    syn: basic; elemental; inborn   *ant: extrinsic*

12. **maxim** (mak´ sim) *n.* an established principle; a truth or rule of
    conduct
    The coach frequently spoke the *maxim*, "A chain is only as strong as its
    weakest link."
    syn: axiom; apothegm; proverb

13. **putrid** (pū´ trid) *adj.* rotten and foul smelling
    We rolled up the car windows to escape the *putrid* smell of a dead skunk
    on the road.
    syn: fetid; rancid; malodorous   *ant: aromatic; fragrant*

14. **servile** (sûr´ vīl) *adj.* submissive; slavish
    The *servile* dog cowered before its intimidating master.
    syn: subservient; ignoble   *ant: haughty; domineering*

15. **apocryphal** (ə pok´ rə fəl) *adj.* of questionable authenticity, but
    widely believed
    Modern historians dismiss the *apocryphal* story that George Washington
    cut down a cherry tree.
    syn: dubious; equivocal; spurious   *ant: genuine; authentic*

Exercise I

Words in Context

From the list below, supply the words needed to complete the paragraph. Some words will not be used.

sybaritic	crepuscular	apocryphal	servile
maxim	internecine	estrange	

1. When Johnny turned fifteen, he inexplicably began a[n] _____ war with his parents. The Smiths asked Johnny how he was able to afford his new laptop computer, and Johnny gave them a[n] _____ story about how it had fallen from the back of a truck. Enraged, they confiscated the computer and ordered Johnny to sit and listen.
    "When your luck runs out and you end up in prison, it will _____ you from your family and friends, and it will limit your options for the future! Your grades are already suffering, and if you make a criminal record for yourself, you'll end up having a low-paying job in which you must be _____ or be fired, while your successful friends enjoy _____ lifestyles by comparison. Is that what you want?"

From the list below, supply the words needed to complete the paragraph. Some words will not be used.

estrange	efficacious	crepuscular	risible
kudos	inundate	intrinsic	

2. Amy arrived at the empty lot just before sundown, when the _____ animals began to emerge from the forest to feed in the grassy field. The new development would soon ruin the _____ value of Amy's childhood stomping grounds, so she wanted to enjoy it one last time before the construction crews arrived. Amy looked over the rows of beech trees and clusters of mountain laurel and thought of the many _____ lessons she had learned there as a child; for example, that poison ivy should not be added to books of pressed leaves. The visit _____ Amy with childhood memories; she would miss having such a[n] _____ way to forget about her many grown-up responsibilities.

From the list below, supply the words needed to complete the paragraph. Some words will not be used.

catharsis	putrid	efficacious	maxim
kudos	internecine	revere	

3. The young captain earned _____ for leading several successful missions in the past, but his troops did not _____ him when he ordered them to march through the _____ mud of a swamp during the most recent training mission. If anyone complained, the captain simply repeated the _____, "We sweat in peace so that we don't bleed in war."

   What many of the soldiers didn't realize was that the captain had planned this rigorous training mission as a[n] _____ to relieve the tension of living in the confining barracks in the months prior to the troops' deployment.

Exercise II

Sentence Completion

Complete the sentence in a way that shows you understand the meaning of the italicized vocabulary word.

1. The *servile* intern withheld any complaints when the cable television magnate told him to...

2. The inspirational posters in the guidance counselor's office listed *maxims* about...

3. Most urban legends are *apocryphal* tales simply meant to...

4. Customers *inundated* the department store with orders when...

5. The *sybaritic* main cabin of the gigantic yacht has all the pleasures of...

6. The company needed an *efficacious* advertising campaign in order to...

7. The antique watch had little material value, but it had enormous *intrinsic* worth because...

8. A hobby or physical activity in the evening can be a genuine *catharsis* for people who...

9. Barb enjoyed *kudos* from her coworkers after she...

10. When the wind blows just the right way, the *putrid* stench of...

11. Flies are not considered *crepuscular* because...

12. Jody *estranged* herself from her family when she...

13. Sergeant Butters didn't *revere* the general well enough to volunteer for...

14. Except for one *risible* scene during the opening credits, the movie...

15. The relatives all believed they were entitled to a huge inheritance, and internecine warfare almost ocurred when...

Exercise III

Roots, Prefixes, and Suffixes

Study the entries and answer the questions that follow.

The root *cant* means "sing."
The root *clam* means "shout."
The prefix *in* means "in," "on," or "onto."
The prefix *re* means "back."
The prefix *ad* means "toward."
The prefix *de* means "down from."
The suffix *ment* means "result of."

1. Using literal translations as guidance, define the following words without using a dictionary.

   A. acclamation   D. incantation
   B. chant   E. canticle
   C. clamorous   F. declamation

2. If *ex* means "out," then the word _____ means "to shout out suddenly."

3. The famous poem by Dante entitled *The Divine Comedy* is divided into chapters called *cantos*. How do you suppose the chapters got this name?

4. The word *enchantment* is also formed with the root *cant*. If *en* means "into," what is the literal definition of this word?

5. List as many words as you can think of that contain the prefix *de*.

Exercise IV

Inference

Complete the sentences by inferring information about the italicized word from its context.

1. If doctors are pleased that Gary's operation proved *efficacious*, then the procedure...

2. Your friends will become *estranged* from you if...

3. During the trial, a judge will usually dismiss *apocryphal* evidence because...

Exercise V

Critical Reading

Below is a passage followed by several multiple-choice questions similar to the ones you will encounter on the ACT. Carefully read the passage and choose the best answer to each of the questions.

The following passage describes the early life of Alexander the Great, King of Macedonia, who constructed the largest western empire of the ancient world during his reign from 336 to 323 B.C.

The father of Alexander the Great, Philip of Macedon, had conquered all of Greece before the elder's assassination in 336 B.C. When Philip died, he left twenty-year-old Alexander with the small task of conquering the Persian Empire. Like a flare that burns with an intense, white-hot flame, Alexander the Great lived fiercely
5 but died young, at the age of thirty-two; however, in his twelve years as king, Alexander built an empire that stretched from Egypt to China.

One may wonder what type of childhood and adolescent influences must have been at work to create such a powerful ruler. At first glance, Alexander was anything but a charismatic leader—he is described as having been of average
10 appearance and of nervous temperament. His one outstanding feature is said to have been his piercing gaze.

Much legend has arisen around Alexander's childhood. He is said to have received a group of envoys from Persia on a day when his father was reviewing his troops, and to have made a more favorable impression on them than his father
15 would have—at the age of six!

Alexander's first teacher, Leonidas, ingrained his own ascetic personality in young Alexander. He imparted a strong work ethic to the boy, which gave Alexander the self-discipline he needed to be a good soldier and a young king. When Alexander traveled with his armies, he lived as his soldiers lived, sleeping
20 on the ground and sharing unsavory rations, foregoing extravagant tents, regal vestments, and luxurious meals that had no purpose on the battlefield.

Alexander's second teacher, Lysimachuis, taught Alexander to appreciate the arts of music, poetry, and drama. His most famous teacher thought, was the Athenian philosopher Aristotle, passed along his knowledge of science, medicine, philosophy,
25 ethics, and politics, all of which contributed to the background that would soon make the thirteen-year-old Alexander a great leader and champion of his people.

One story that demonstrates young Alexander's precocious nature is that of Alexander and his horse, Bucephalus. Philonicus of Thessaly presented a horse to sell to Philip, but none of Philip's farmhands could handle the wild Bucephalus.
30 Alexander noticed that the animal was afraid of its own shadow, so he wagered 13 talents—the price of the horse—that he could tame it. Philip accepted the wager, and Alexander quickly collected his prize after leading the horse toward the sun, so that the animal could not see its shadow, mounting it, and riding it.

Not all of the tales associated with Alexander's youth are as charming as that of the
35 tale of Bucephalus. Philip took several concubines during his reign, one of whom was
named Cleopatra and was the daughter of a Macedonian aristocrat (not the Cleopatra
who ruled Egypt. During the wedding feast, Cleopatra's uncle, Attalus, suggested that
Philip and Cleopatra produce a pure Macedonian heir (Alexander's mother, Olympias,
was an Albanian who practiced Dionysian rituals that were not commonly condoned
40 in Macedonia; Alexander was not considered to be a pure Macedonian). Alexander
took great offense to the suggestion, a brawl ensued, and a rift grew between
Alexander and his father that lasted until Philip was assassinated in 336.

Alexander is often described as the ruler who accomplished more in twelve
years than anyone else had accomplished in an entire lifetime. Alexander, like
45 many princes, had a superior education in arts, sciences, and military strategy, but
perhaps it was the unconventional education—that which a dysfunctional family
presents—that somehow fueled Alexander's ambition. Whatever the deciding
factors, Alexander undoubtedly is remembered as one of the most powerful military
leaders in the history of the world.

1. Which word would be the best antonym for *ascetic* as it appears in line 16
    of the passage?
    A. cynical
    B. austere
    C. cheap
    D. indulgent

2. According to the passage, which of the following was probably NOT a
    factor in the development of Alexander's personality?
    F. Philip's dislike of Olympias' religious beliefs
    G. Leonidas' belief in the denial of the self
    H. Alexander's skill with horses
    J. Aristotle's teachings in ethics

3. As used in line 21, *vestments* most nearly means
    A. robes.
    B. weaponry.
    C. goblets.
    D. scrolls.

4. The best title for the passage would be
    F. An Imperialistic Mind.
    G. Legends of Alexander's Youth.
    H. The Youth of a Warrior King.
    J. Aristotle and Alexander.

5. Which of the following statements is not true about the passage?
    A. The passage is written in third person point of view.
    B. The passage asserts that Alexander's education contributed to his career.
    C. The passage is rigidly academic and written in a formal style.
    D. The passage provides a favorable portrayal of Alexander.

6. Which choice best describes the tone of the passage?
    F. solemn and virtuous
    G. irreverent but unbiased
    H. sensationalistic but positive
    J. humorous but evasive

7. The passage suggests that the assassination of Philip was
    A. a result of Philip's conflict with Alexander.
    B. probably a part of Alexander's plan to become emperor.
    C. not connected to Alexander's resentment toward Philip.
    D. retribution for Bucephalus' slight against Alexander.

8. Which of the following details is not mentioned as a formative element of Alexander's successful rise?
    F. skillful communication
    G. science and philosophy
    H. adaptation to harsh conditions
    J. hand to hand combat proficiency

9. *Talents*, as used in paragraph 6, are probably
    A. weight.
    B. currency.
    C. references.
    D. skills.

10. Which answer best explains the purpose of paragraph 6?
    F. It demonstrates the link between understanding animals and leadership.
    G. The story is an entertaining break in the otherwise dry passage.
    H. Paragraph 6 is a parable about the virtue of patience.
    J. The paragraph suggests that Alexander's wisdom exceeded his age.

Vocabulary
Power Plus
for the
ACT
Vocabulary,
Reading, and Writing
Exercises for High Scores

Lesson Five

1. **consternation** (kon stər nā′ shən) *n.* alarming dismay or concern
    The announcement of a pop quiz caused *consternation* among the
    students.
    syn: bewilderment; shock; trepidation   *ant: composure; tranquility*

2. **anomaly** (ə nom′ ə lē) *n.* a deviation from the norm; an odd or
         peculiar occurrence
    The sailor immediately notified the captain when he saw an *anomaly* on
    the sonar screen.
    syn: eccentricity; irregularity; oddity

3. **vitriolic** (vit rē ol′ ik) *adj.* harsh in tone; bitterly critical
    The critic's *vitriolic* review of the new film prompted thousands of
    letters praising the movie.
    syn: caustic; offensive; scathing   *ant: flattering; genial*

4. **preamble** (prē′ am bəl) *n.* a preliminary statement; an introduction
    After reciting a long-winded *preamble*, the lawyer finally presented some
    pertinent facts.
    syn: prologue; preface; opening   *ant: epilogue; finale*

5. **coterie** (kō′ tə rē) *n.* a small group of people who share interests and
         meet frequently
    Virginia Woolf was a member of the Bloomsbury Group, a *coterie* of
    English authors respected for its talent, but ridiculed for its arrogance.
    syn: circle; clique; society

6. **expiate** (ek′ spē āt) *v.* to make amends for
    Johnny mowed the neighbors' lawn free of charge all summer to *expiate*
    the guilt he felt for breaking their front window with a baseball.
    syn: atone; correct; rectify

7. **compendium** (kəm pen′ dē əm) *n.* a list or collection of items
    Jen perused a *compendium* of antique toys to find the value of an old doll.
    syn: compilation; index; anthology

8. **comprise** (kəm prīz′) *v.* to include or consist of; contain
    Canada *comprises* ten provinces and three territories.
    syn: constitute; encompass; incorporate   *ant: exclude; lack*

9. **eidetic** (ī det´ ik) *adj.* pertaining to extraordinarily detailed and vivid recall
The author attempted to describe the *eidetic* scenes in his head.
syn: vivid   *ant: vague*

10. **innocuous** (i nok´ yōō əs) *adj.* harmless
The assassin wore a disguise and a smile to make himself look like an *innocuous* old man.
syn: inoffensive; innocent   *ant: injurious*

11. **foist** (foist) *v.* to pass off as genuine or valuable
The secret service arrested the man who *foisted* counterfeit $20 bills off on the unsuspecting country.
syn: fob

12. **plethora** (pleth´ ər ə) *n.* an overabundance; excess
The library has a *plethora* of information about most any subject imaginable.
syn: surplus   *ant: deficiency; shortage; paucity*

13. **flippancy** (flip´ ənt cē) *n.* disrespect
His *flippancy* in class often got him sent to the principal's office.
syn: irreverence; rudeness; impertinence   *ant: respect; reverence*

14. **incongruous** (in kong´ grōō əs) *adj.* incompatible; unsuitable for the situation
Ed's *incongruous* joke about policemen ensured he would get a speeding ticket.
syn: discordant; improper   *ant: compatible; fitting*

15. **disconcert** (dis kən sûrt´) *v.* to frustrate; confuse
The lengthy calculus problem on the quiz *disconcerted* Nancy.
syn: agitate; fluster; perplex   *ant: enlighten; comfort; encourage*

Exercise I

Words in Context

From the list below, supply the words needed to complete the paragraph. Some words will not be used.

foist	consternation	coterie	comprise
plethora	innocuous	eidetic	

1.   Each month, a[n] _____ of radio-controlled model airplane enthusiasts meets at an open field at the Ames farm, weather permitting (to the group's _____, rain canceled two meetings this summer already). The group _____ aviation fans from all over the county, and members with years of aeronautical experience offer a[n] _____ of knowledge and experience to amateurs in the club. The farmer who owns the field sees the meetings as _____, as long as no one crashes a plane into his house or his livestock.

From the list below, supply the words needed to complete the paragraph. Some words will not be used.

foist	vitriolic	innocuous	preamble
anomaly	flippancy	expiate	

2.   Heather made a[n] _____ phone call when she realized that the crooked electronics shop had just _____ a cheap replica of a brand-name digital camera on her, but charged her the price of the genuine camera. No one answered the phone at the store, so Heather went, in person, to deal with her concerns. When Heather entered the store, the owner confronted her. In his insulting _____, he scolded Heather for her _____ in spreading such nasty, unfounded rumors about the business; then, quietly, so the other customers didn't hear, the owner offered to _____ his offense by offering Heather a more expensive camera at no additional cost. Heather simply shook her head and demanded her money back.

From the list below, supply the words needed to complete the paragraph. Some words will not be used.

anomaly   coterie   compendium   expiate
eidetic   incongruous   disconcert

3.   Allen has a[n] _____ memory when it comes to remembering faces, so it was quite a[n] _____ when a stranger asked, "Don't you know me?" and Allen was forced to say "No." The stranger issued a simple, "You'll remember," before leaving Allen's store. The visit was _____ to Allen; he hated having a[n] _____ gap in the memory he often boasted about. That evening at home, Allen perused every _____ of customer names and addresses he could find, hoping to spark his memory.

Exercise II

Sentence Completion

Complete the sentence in a way that shows you understand the meaning of the italicized vocabulary word.

1. Ed could not get over his *consternation* when he saw…

2. In a *preamble* to the novel, the author writes…

3. The museum director has a *compendium* that categorizes…

4. That spider is *innocuous*, so…

5. Private Miller quickly departed from his usual *flippancy* when…

6. Ben saw that discussing evolution was *disconcerting* to his students, so he…

7. The *anomaly* in the clouds turned out to be…

8. To gain membership in the *coterie* of artists, applicants had to…

9. The average dinner salad usually *comprises*…

10. On the street corner, a shady-looking man tried to *foist*…

11. Mike's fear at the sight of blood was *incongruous* with his…

12. Lyle received a *vitriolic* lecture from his teacher for…

13. Heidi could not *expiate* her negative feelings about the divorce, so she…

14. The old man forgot many things, but he still had an *eidetic* memory of the day he…

15. After a lengthy search, the starving castaways were thrilled to discover that the tiny island offered a *plethora* of…

Exercise III

Roots, Prefixes, and Suffixes

Study the entries and answer the questions that follow.

The root *ject* means "throw."
The root *tract* means "drag" or "draw."
The prefix *con* means "together."
The prefix *de* means "down."
The prefix *in* means "not."
The prefix *pro* means "forward."

1. Using literal translations as guidance, define the following words without using a dictionary.

   A. conjecture   D. injection
   B. dejected   E. detract
   C. intractable   F. protracted

2. What does a *projector* literally do?

3. When the prefix *ex*, which means "out," is added to the root *ject*, a letter drops out. What word do we get from this prefix and root?

4. Something that *draws* people *together* legally is a _____.

5. List as many words as you can think of that contain the root *ject*.

6. List as many words as you can think of that contain the prefix *con*.

Exercise IV

Inference

Complete the sentences by inferring information about the italicized word from its context.

1. If the editor's *vitriolic* critique of the novel brings the writer to tears, then the editor must think that...

2. A cheese merchant might have a *compendium* that lists...

3. If a doctor finds an *anomaly* on someone's X-ray, then the patient will probably want to...

Exercise V

Writing

Here is a writing prompt similar to the one you will find on the writing portion of the ACT.

Imagine that a miracle spice has been recently discovered which, if ingested, adds 300 years to the average human lifespan. There is enough of the spice in existence to supply almost everyone in the nation with a single dose, rendering them virtually immortal, compared to the humans who do not receive the treatment.

The spice is too valuable a resource to simply discard—its lifesaving value alone could, temporarily at least, virtually stop death in the nation. There is no way to dilute the spice so that it can be distributed to a larger population—only the maximum dose yields the full effect.

You, as the leader of the free world, have the responsibility of deciding what to do with the existing supply of the spice. In a well-written essay, describe your plan for handling the distribution of the spice, and defend your decision. Include who will, or should, receive it, how it is to be managed, or if there should be a selection process for the recipients.

Be sure to account for many possibilities concerning the discovery: No one not yet born can receive it, other nations would want some and be willing to go to war to obtain it, people of power and money will demand greater access to it, as will the criminal element of society.

Thesis: Write a one-sentence response to the above assignment. Make certain this sentence offers a clear statement of your position.

Example: Because the longevity spice is something that humans have desired for thousands of years and because of its priceless value, a selection process must be instituted to assure that those in greatest need of it—the elderly, the terminally ill, and the members of the military—receive it first.

_____

_____

Organizational Plan: If your thesis is the point on which you want to end, where does your essay need to begin? List the points of development that are inevitable in leading your reader from your beginning point to your end point. This list is your outline.

1. _____

2. _____

3. _____

Draft: Use your thesis as both your beginning and your end. Following your outline, write a good first draft of your essay. Remember to support all of your points with examples, facts, references to reading, etc.

Review and revise: Exchange essays with a classmate. Using the scoring guide for Sentence Formation and Variety on page 243, score your partner's essay (while he or she scores yours). Focus on sentence structure and the use of language conventions. If necessary, rewrite your essay to improve the sentence structure and your use of language.

Exercise VI

English Practice

Identifying Sentence Errors

Identify the errors in the following sentences. Choose the answer that fixes the error. If the sentence contains no error, select NO CHANGE.

1. <u>Everyone in the office laughs</u> at Betty, who used to work here, because she said she was the smartest person who had ever worked for the company.
    A. NO CHANGE
    B. Everyone in the office is laughing
    C. Everyone in the office laughed
    D. Everyone in the office can laugh

2. The man in the water <u>shouted, "Help!" when</u> he started to get tired from all the swimming he done.
    F. NO CHANGE
    G. shouted "help," when
    H. shouted, "Help" when
    J. shouted "Help"! when

3. If you dig <u>further and deeper</u> into Bill's reason for embezzling the money from his father's company, you will see that the crime began when the older man removed him from the will.
   A. NO CHANGE
   B. farther and deeper
   C. far and deep
   D. further and more deeply

4. The <u>children all of who</u> had all been playing noisily in their backyard, fled to the safety of the back porch at the first sound of thunder, which is exactly what their parents had told them to do.
   F. NO CHANGE
   G. children, all of who
   H. children all of whom
   J. children, all of whom

5. <u>The time has come my fellow citizens, to</u> confront the problem of poverty at a national level.
   A. NO CHANGE
   B. The time has come, my fellow citizens, to
   C. The time has come my fellow citizens to
   D. My fellow citizens the time has come to

Improving Sentences
The underlined portion of each sentence below contains some flaw. Select the answer that best corrects the flaw.

6. The young girl <u>wanted to go to see whoever her parents wanted to see, and whenever they wanted to go.</u>
   F. wanted to see whoever her parents wanted, and whenever they wanted.
   G. wanted to visit whomever her parents wanted, whenever they wanted to go.
   H. wanted to go to see whomever her parents wanted to see, and whenever the parents wanted to go.
   J. wanted to go to see whoever her parents wanted to see, whenever they wanted to.

7. <u>The butterflies, which emerged from their cocoons this year, will</u> not be the same ones that migrate to Mexico for the winter.
   A. The butterflies, that emerged from their cocoons this year, will
   B. The butterflies, which climbed out of their cocoons this year, will
   C. Every butterfly, which emerged from their cocoons this year, will
   D. The butterflies that emerged from their cocoons this year will

8. <u>Everybody involved in the student plays last Saturday and Sunday are to receive</u> an extra day to study before finals.
    F. Everyone involved in the student plays last Saturday and Sunday are to receive
    G. Everybody involved in the student plays last Saturday and Sunday is to receive
    H. Everybody involved in the student plays last Saturday and Sunday will have received
    J. Everybody in the student plays last Saturday and Sunday are to receive

9. <u>Playing in the park, the stormy weather ruined the childrens' game of dodge ball.</u>
    A. The stormy weather ruined the childrens' game of dodge ball playing in the park.
    B. Playing in the park, the stormy weather ruined the children's game of dodge ball.
    C. The stormy weather ruined the childrens' game of dodge ball who were playing in the park.
    D. The stormy weather ruined the children's dodge ball game in the park.

10. <u>Anyone who comes to the football game wearing a player's T-shirt receive</u> 50% off the price of admission.
    F. Anyone, who comes to the football game wearing a player's T-shirt, will receive
    G. Everybody who come to the football game wearing a player's T-shirt will receive
    H. Anyone who comes to the football game wearing a player's T-shirt receives
    J. Anyone who comes to the football game, and also who wears a player's T-shirt shall receive

Lesson Six

1. **sectarian** (sek târ´ ē ən) *adj.* narrowly confined to a particular group
    Members of the *sectarian* cult gave no thought to the beliefs of outsiders.
    syn: insular; dogmatic　　　　　　　*ant: tolerant*

2. **peregrination** (per i grə nāt´ shən) *n.* travel by walking
    Vince planned a summer of *peregrination* throughout Europe.
    syn: trekking; exploration

3. **accoutrement** (ə kōō´ trə mənt) *n.* an accessory item of dress or
        equipment
    Various *accoutrements* dangled from the workbelt of the telephone
    repairman.
    syn: device; gear

4. **contrive** (kən trīv´) *v.* to plan cleverly; to devise
    After four days in captivity, Steve *contrived* an escape plan that could not
    fail.
    syn: concoct; design; engineer

5. **hubris** (hyōō´ bris) *n.* overbearing pride; arrogance
    Hubris is the character flaw found in many tragic heroes.
    syn: conceit; smugness; pompousness　　　*ant: humility; modesty*

6. **platitude** (plat´ i tōōd) *n.* an obvious remark; a cliché
    The two candidates offered plenty of *platitudes,* but no practical solutions.
    syn: maxim; truism; banality

7. **venerate** (ven´ ə rāt) *v.* to respect or revere
    Young scholars often *venerate* the ideas of the great philosophers.
    syn: glorify; treasure　　　　　　*ant: abhor; despise*

8. **scullion** (skul´ yən) *n.* a servant for menial tasks
    Scullions scrubbed the castle floors for hours prior to the king's feast.
    syn: peon; toiler　　　　　　*ant: patrician; aristocrat*

9. **quotidian** (kwō ti´ dē ən) *adj.* everyday; commonplace
    Earthquakes were *quotidian* events for the people living near the volcano.
    syn: ordinary; routine　　　　　*ant: rare; uncommon*

10. **prognosticate** (präg năs´ tə kāt) *v.* to predict
    Meteorologists are attempting to *prognosticate* the path of the hurricane.
    syn: forecast; foreshadow

11. **antediluvian** (an ti də lōō´ vē ən) *adj.* extremely old; antiquated
    Especially tall structures were rare in the ancient world because
    antediluvian architecture could not withstand the enormous forces.
    syn: ancient; archaic   *ant: modern; new*

12. **stringent** (strin´ jənt) *adj.* restrictive; imposing demanding standards
    The dynamite factory imposed *stringent* safety rules to prevent any
    catastrophe.
    syn: severe; rigid; inflexible   *ant: lenient; flexible*

13. **haughty** (hô´ tē) *adj.* condescendingly proud; arrogant
    The *haughty* boy thought that his family's wealth made him better than
    other students.
    syn: conceited; snobbish; supercilious *ant: humble; modest*

14. **sanctimonious** (sangk tə mō´ nə əs) *adj.* showing false piety or
    righteousness
    The *sanctimonious* landlord made public contributions to charities, but
    threatened his tenants with eviction if they didn't pay the rent on time.
    syn: hypocritical; specious   *ant: humble; modest*

15. **imbroglio** (im brōl´ yō) *n.* a difficult and embarrassing situation
    His infatuation with a married co-worker led to an *imbroglio* at the office
    picnic.
    syn: predicament   *ant: peace; serenity*

Exercise I

Words in Context

From the list below, supply the words needed to complete the paragraph. Some words will not be used.

imbroglio	quotidian	sanctimonious	scullion
peregrination	hubris	prognosticate	

1. There was a[n] _____ at the garage. A customer arrived and demanded to see his car, after having been told that the repairs were nearly finished, but found that the work had not even begun.

   "Two weeks ago, you said that the job would take three or four days, but that _____ was wrong," the customer sarcastically said to Jane, the receptionist. "Give me the keys; I'll take my car to a different garage." Jane complied, still smiling as usual; she never worried about losing an occasional customer, though she did feel bad about mistakenly telling the customer that his car was finished. Angry customers were a[n] _____ occurrence in the auto repair business; most people have a tendency to become emotional when they receive bills for hundreds or even thousands of dollars, especially for repairs to cars that are still relatively new. Jane knew that every garage in town was overloaded. Upon hearing the customer's story, the other garage would offer some _____ criticism of Jane's garage, accept the job, and then do exactly what Jane's garage did, since the car required a tedious repair that yielded little profit. The whole frustrating process simply causes many drivers to abandon their cars and resort to _____ as their primary form of transportation.

From the list below, supply the words needed to complete the paragraph. Some words will not be used.

platitude	haughty	contrive	stringent
sectarian	quotidian	scullions	

2. After reviewing the pamphlets for the private school, Veronica's parents thought that the school might be too _____ because of its religious affiliation, but they favored the _____ educational requirements to which the students were held.

   Veronica assumed that the private school would be full of _____, rich children who probably treated middle-class people like _____. She was about to _____ a way to get out of going to the school, but at the last minute, she decided to give it a try.

From the list below, supply the words needed to complete the paragraph. Some words will not be used.

accoutrement	hubris	platitude	prognosticate
venerate	antediluvian	contrive	

3. Most people rendered a typical _____ to Tracey before the triathlon, such as "Good luck," or "Pace yourself," but Tracey's mother, who _____ famous women and _____ conquerors such as Cleopatra, simply said, "Win the race or don't bother starting it." Tracey smiled as she removed her watch, earrings, and other _____ before confidently walking to the triathlon's registration booth. Tracey also hoped that her own _____ hadn't clouded her own expectations of how well she would do in the race; she was in excellent shape, but so were the other two hundred competitors.

Exercise II

Sentence Completion

Complete the sentence in a way that shows you understand the meaning of the italicized vocabulary word.

1. The thief found himself in an *imbroglio* when he...

2. Our *sectarian* neighbors seldom speak to us because they...

3. The corrupt police commissioner often made the *sanctimonious* claim that he...

4. *Peregrination* was the most common form of transportation before...

5. Kevin left the country club because he didn't like the way in which *haughty* members...

6. Ashley bought the new dress, but she still needed *accoutrements* such as...

7. Carol, the secretary, began to feel like the boss's *scullion* when he told her to...

8. Cindy *venerates* the huge walnut tree on the property line, but Bill, her neighbor, would like to...

9. Rachel warned her son that his *hubris*, left unchecked, would...

10. Nathan was tired of watching *quotidian* television sitcoms, so he...

11. Rabbits and woodchucks were eating the vegetables in the garden, so Bob *contrived* a way to...

12. Despite the claims of being able to *prognosticate* the future, most fortune-tellers and physics...

13. Watching a movie with our father is difficult because he feels obligated to voice some *platitude* every time...

14. Dana was certain that she could meet the *stringent* training requirements of...

15. People of the remote mountain village retained *antediluvian* traditions that...

Exercise III

Roots, Prefixes, and Suffixes

Study the entries and answer the questions that follow.

The prefix *pre* means "before."
The root *bene* means "good" or "well."
The root *optim* means "best."
The root *dict* means "speech."
The root *ven* means "come."
The prefix *contra* means "against."
The prefix *con* means "together."

1. *Using literal translations as guidance, define the following words without using a dictionary.*

    A. contradiction   D. optimal
    B. optimistic   E. contravene
    C. convene   F. benediction

2. The root *male* has the opposite meaning of the root *bene*. What, then, is a *malediction*?

3. What do you suppose a *venue* is?

4. If you *talk* about something *before* it happens, then you might be making a[n] _____.

5. List as many words as you can think of that contain the root *dict*.

6. List as many words as you can think of that contain the root *bene*.

Exercise IV

Inference

Complete the sentences by inferring information about the italicized word from its context.

1. A university might have *stringent* academic requirements for admission to ensure that...

2. During a *quotidian* visit to the grocery store, you probably wouldn't expect to...

3. Devoted fans might *venerate* their idol long after...

Exercise V

Critical Reading

Below is a reading passage followed by several multiple-choice questions similar to the ones you will encounter on the ACT. Carefully read the passage and choose the best answer for each of the questions.

The following passage describes the characteristics of the Maya, Inca, and Aztec cultures of Central and South America.

To many, the mere mention of Mayan, Aztec, or Incan civilization evokes thoughts of great, flat-topped pyramids of mysterious origin, secret cities perched on remote mountaintops, and booby-trapped temples brimming with treasure-hoards of gold. Indeed, impressions have not changed much since the age of the
5   Spanish explorers, who, despite intentions of conquest, were also mystified by the cryptic civilizations of Mesoamerica and South America. Explorers may not have found the mythical golden city of El Dorado, but they did find three amazing cultures, each with unique characteristics.

Mayan civilization, often considered to be the most exalted and mysterious of
10   the three, inhabited the Yucatan Peninsula of Eastern Mexico as long ago as 2,600 B.C. Emerging from a collection of city-states with no central government, the Maya reached a cultural peak between A.D. 250 and 900. The Maya, who developed an astrological calendar that allowed them to grow crops in poor soil, were originally thought to be a peaceful people, but archaeologists have since determined that
15   intertribal warfare brought about their decline. Mayans, like the Aztecs and Incas, also practiced human sacrifice. Ancient pyramids inscribed with weathered glyphs and characters from the most advanced ancient alphabet in the western hemisphere now sit abandoned, obscured by centuries of jungle growth. Mayan descendents still inhabit the Yucatan, but the technology, religion, and practices of the ancient
20   civilization must now be slowly exhumed and catalogued by archaeologists.

The Aztecs, noted perhaps most often for their penchant for battle and human sacrifice, composed the second-largest pre-Columbian civilization in central America. Originally a nomadic society inhabiting the central basin of Mexico, the various tribes who identified themselves as Aztec settled in the marshy region near
25   Lake Texcoco and, in 1325, founded the city of Tenochtitlan at the present site of Mexico City. Despite vicious religious practices, the Aztec demonstrated ingenuity by inventing an innovative farming technique to grow crops among the 30 canals of Tenochtitlan. Farmers built chinampas, or artificial, fertile islands floating in canals, to grow crops of beans, peppers, avocados, tomatoes, and, most important,
30   corn. Ironically, the seemingly bloodthirsty culture, when not participating in an estimated 20,000 human sacrifices a year, took great interest in the beauty of nature; Aztecs, who lacked plows or beasts of burden, took the time to grow beautiful flowers strictly for decoration. Before falling to the Spanish in 1521, the Aztecs left several permanent contributions to history and to the explorers of the
35   New World: chocolate, derived from indigenous cacao beans; tomatoes, potatoes,

and numerous other vegetables that have long become staples to the rest of the world; and, as testament to the artisans among the Aztecs, an accurate, 24-ton limestone calendar that took more than fifty years to construct.

Incas, whose feats of engineering baffle modern architects, dominated the west
40 coast of South America from 1300 to 1535. Like the Aztecs, the Incas practiced human sacrifice and lacked a written language; however, the Incas made up for language shortcomings with advanced architecture and a complex government. In addition to having the most advanced medical and surgical techniques of the ancient Americas, the Incas constructed more than 12,000 miles of roadway
45 and aqueducts to supply taxpaying and labor-contributing tribes throughout the empire. The precise, intricate stonemasonry of Incan pyramids, fortresses, and walls commands the respect of even modern masons. Incan architecture still dots the Andean mountains and highlands as the timeless endeavors of a lost people.

So, despite the achievements and predominance of the two civilizations intact
50 after Columbus arrived in the New World, they found themselves at the mercy of the Spaniards during the sixteenth century. Hernando Cortez, who sought control of the Aztec Empire, or Mexican Empire, began his quest in 1519 by forming alliances with tribes who were displeased with the leadership of Montezuma II in Tenochtitlan. Cortez went to the city and took Montezuma hostage, taking
55 advantage of the fact that Aztecs thought that the Spaniards were descendents of their god, Quetzalcoatl, and had come to fulfill a prophecy. Montezuma was killed during a short uprising in 1521 while instructing the Aztecs to make peace with the Spaniards. The Spaniards were forced to retreat from the city, but they soon regrouped and besieged the Aztec capital. After the eventual surrender, Cortez
60 burned the city and destroyed the greatest monuments of Aztec culture.

The Incan Empire shared a fate similar to that of the Aztec, but at the hands of a conquistador more sinister than Cortez. Francisco Pizarro, motivated by legends of treasure, captured the Incan ruler Atahualpa during their first meeting. Atahualpa offered a ransom for himself that consisted of a roomful of gold. Atahualpa revealed
65 the location of the treasure to Pizarro, and Pizarro promptly executed the ruler and seized control of Cuzco, the Incan capital. Pizarro was eventually killed by his own people, but the Incan Empire was forever lost.

Aztecs, Incas, and Mayans who escaped the iron swords and gunpowder of the Europeans instead suffered the old world diseases that accompanied the explorers.
70 Entire tribes vanished as smallpox, scarlet fever, and influenza decimated the native population of the Americas. Those who survived were forced to abandon their customs and live beneath Spanish rule for the next three centuries.

Millions of tourists now visit Mexico and Peru to see the remnants of the Mayan, Aztec, and Inca civilizations. Though weathered or overgrown, the relics stand as
75 permanent markers of the ingenuity and art of the pre-Columbian civilizations. Archaeologists and treasure hunters scour newly discovered burial platforms and caves in search of knowledge that might contribute to the modern understanding of the lost cultures, and also, undoubtedly, to find relics made of that one material valued by both the ancient and modern worlds: gold.

1. The purpose of this passage is to
   A. explain how Spanish explorers decimated other cultures.
   B. demonstrate the differences among three early cultures.
   C. show early cultural advances.
   D. show the relationships among the three cultures.

2. The term *Mesoamerica* most nearly means
   F. South America.
   G. coastal America.
   H. prehistoric America.
   J. Middle America.

3. It is ironic that the Aztecs grew flowers because
   A. flowers do not grow well where the Aztecs lived.
   B. flower nurseries are indicative of a society with leisure time.
   C. the Aztecs were violent and warlike.
   D. Aztecs had no calendar to determine the best time to grow flowers.

4. The term *pre-Columbian* describes
   F. all civilization that preceded the nation of Colombia.
   G. everything before the year in which the Inca Empire fell.
   H. the new name that Cortez gave to Tenochtitlan.
   J. the time before Columbus arrived in the Americas in 1492.

5. The word *staple* (line 36) most nearly means
   A. to fasten.
   B. a basic dietary item.
   C. a luxurious food.
   D. an overabundance.

6. Which answer is implied by the following quotation (lines 44-46)?

   "...the Incas constructed more than 12,000 miles of roadway and aqueducts to supply taxpaying...tribes throughout the empire."

   F. The Incas had some type of central government.
   G. Incan roadways were elevated high above the ground.
   H. High taxes probably accelerated the fall of the Incan Empire.
   J. Incas wasted resources on building roadways.

7. Unlike the Aztecs and Incas, the Mayans had
    A. knowledge of planting crops.
    B. a written language.
    C. human sacrifice.
    D. a calendar.

8. The passage contains no details about the Spanish conquering the Mayans because
    F. all Mayan people mysteriously disappeared in A.D. 1450.
    G. the Portuguese conquered the Mayans, and this passage focuses on the Spanish.
    H. Mayan civilization declined before the Europeans arrived.
    J. Europe had no interests in the Yucatan peninsula.

9. Which choice would be the best title for this passage?
    A. Human Sacrifice in Three Civilizations
    B. Aztec, Inca, and Maya in South America
    C. Three Lost Civilizations
    D. The History of Ancient Mexico and Parts of South America

10. The author of this passage would probably agree that
    F. explorers should not have interfered with the Mesoamerican or South American cultures.
    G. human sacrifice is an acceptable practice.
    H. the Aztecs were far more advanced than the Incas.
    J. the Spaniards were devious in the way they conquered the Aztecs and Incas.

Vocabulary
Power Plus
for the
ACT
Vocabulary,
Reading, and Writing
Exercises for High Scores

Lesson Seven

1. **gibberish** (jib´ ər ish) *n.* nonsense; unintelligible speech
   A foreign language might sound like *gibberish* until you learn key words and phrases.
   syn: babble; chatter; prattle

2. **inimical** (i nim´ i kəl) *adj.* unfriendly; hostile; injurious
   The stranger's *inimical* voice made me wonder if I had done something wrong.
   syn: mean; malicious; harmful   *ant: encouraging; flattering*

3. **nexus** (nek´ səs) *n.* a link, tie, or bond
   The desire for acceptance by others is a *nexus* for all humankind.
   syn: connection; correlation   *ant: disruption; gap*

4. **coeval** (kō ē´ vəl) *adj.* of the same time period
   Scientists assert that the two ancient, *coeval* civilizations, though thousands of miles apart, were aware of each other.
   syn: contemporaneous

5. **dilatory** (di´ lə tōr ē) *adj.* tending to delay or procrastinate
   The teacher warned the *dilatory* students that any paper turned in after the deadline would be an instant failure.
   syn: dallying; laggard; unhurried   *ant: diligent; prompt*

6. **convoluted** (kon´ və lŏŏt əd) *adj.* complicated; intricate
   Few people in class understood the teacher's *convoluted* explanation of the problem.
   syn: involved; jumbled   *ant: simple; obvious*

7. **entreat** (en trēt´) *v.* to earnestly request or petition
   At the supermarket, the child first *entreated* his mother for the candy bar, and then cried for it.
   syn: importune; implore   *ant: demand*

8. **anecdote** (an´ ik dōt) *n.* a short account of an incident
   New parents often share *anecdotes* about their children.
   syn: narrative

9. **incumbent** (in kum´ bənt) *adj.* obligatory; necessary
It is *incumbent* on the night watchman to stay awake during his shift.
syn: required; essential   *ant: voluntary; unnecessary*

10. **churlish** (chûr´ lish) *adj.* boorish or vulgar
The wild cowboys' *churlish* behavior offended the genteel townspeople.
syn: uncouth; rude; surly   *ant: courteous; polished; civil*

11. **promulgate** (prom´ əl gāt) *v.* to announce; to make known
During the drought, the city *promulgated* strict rules about water usage.
syn: declare; exhibit

12. **staid** (stād) *adj.* showing dignity and often strait-laced propriety
The *staid* general spoke softly, seldom dismounted his horse, and never smiled.
syn: composed; serious; solemn   *ant: agitated; excited; nervous*

13. **livid** (liv´ id) *adj.* extremely angry
When I was brought home by the police, my father was *livid*; he yelled at me for hours.
syn: enraged; furious; fuming   *ant: contented; pleased*

14. **lurid** (lŏŏr´ id) *adj.* shocking; explicit
The *lurid* crime appeared in every newspaper in the city.
syn: sensational; extreme   *ant: dull; boring; mediocre*

15. **cogent** (kō´ jənt) *adj.* convincing; reasonable
Bert's *cogent* justification for a new desk convinced management to buy one for him.
syn: compelling; pertinent; influential   *ant: ineffective; weak*

Exercise I

Words in Context

From the list below, supply the words needed to complete the paragraph. Some words will not be used.

gibberish	**livid**	**staid**	**promulgate**
cogent	**incumbent**	**nexus**	

1. The boss was _____ after he learned about the accounting error that cost the company thousands of dollars, but he vowed to remain calm and _____ while he sought a[n] _____ explanation for the mistake. This was the second major error in six months, and it was _____ on the company to find the source of the problem. When confronted, the nervous accountant quickly listed possible excuses for what might have gone wrong.

    "Spare me your _____ and tell me exactly where the error originated," ordered the boss.

From the list below, supply the words needed to complete the paragraph. Some words will not be used.

lurid	**cogent**	**anecdote**	**entreat**
inimical	**nexus**	**coeval**	

2. When the children asked their father about an old, abandoned cabin in the forest behind their house, he responded with a[n] _____ about the day he discovered it, when he, too, was eleven years old.

    "Enos, a[n] _____ hermit, once lived in that shack," said father, "and he used to shoot at anyone who dared to trespass on his property. The old man, rumored to be an escaped convict hiding from the law, was the last member of a family _____ with the bootlegging industry that flourished in these woods during the Prohibition Era."

    The _____ story so fascinated the children that they had to venture into the forest to look at the rotting timbers of the overgrown cabin once again. The father's memory was now a[n] _____ that connected the children's generation to a lost era, and the children planned to access that link more often in the future.

From the list below, supply the words needed to complete the paragraph. Some words will not be used.

dilatory	convoluted	entreat	gibberish
churlish	promulgate	nexus	

3.   Roger _____ his teacher for more time, but she told him to put his pencil down and hand in his test like everyone else. Once again, Roger's _____ approach to test-taking had resulted in another incomplete exam, but he blamed it on the _____ word problems on which he had spent too much time. He stood and _____ his obvious failure to the rest of the class by making the whistling sound of a bomb falling from the sky and then exploding on the ground. The teacher then asked Roger to take his _____ behavior outside.

Exercise II

Sentence Completion

Complete the sentence in a way that shows you understand the meaning of the italicized vocabulary word.

1.   Craig was *livid* after learning that…

2.   Maggie failed to give Sam a *cogent* reason for…

3.   Aaron could speak only *gibberish* after having his wisdom teeth removed because…

4.   Dave *entreated* his messy roommate to…

5.   The athlete remained *staid*, despite…

6.   The *lurid* crime of Irene's next-door neighbor…

7.   Getting an occasional checkup is *incumbent* on anyone who…

8.   The detective's voice had an *inimical* tone when he…

9.   At the class reunion, alumni shared *anecdotes* about…

10. Dinosaurs were not *coeval* with humankind, so early humans did not need to…

11. When the teacher saw the *churlish* message on Gary's tee shirt, she told him to…

12. Shawn knew that his *dilatory* work habits would…

13. The government *promulgated* the false concept that…

14. The teacher asked the student to revise the *convoluted* essay so that…

15. A song that never seems to fade in popularity is sometimes called a generational *nexus* because…

Exercise III

Roots, Prefixes, and Suffixes

Study the entries and answer the questions that follow.

The root *spect* means "look."
The roots *vid* and *vis* mean "see."
The root *aud* means "hear."
The prefix *circum* means "around."
The prefix *in* can mean "not," "upon," or "against."

1. Without using a dictionary, define the following words.

   A. auditory   D. spectator
   B. circumspect   E. invidious
   C. inaudible   F. spectrum

2. A place specifically designed for *hearing* music, speeches, or recitals, is called a[n] _____.

3. What do you suppose a *specter* is?

4. List as many words as you can think of that contain the root *spect*.

5. List as many words as you can think of that contain the root *vis*.

Exercise IV

Inference

Complete the sentences by inferring information about the italicized word from its context.

1. If you miss an important exam, you might *entreat* the teacher to...

2. Someone who gives you an *inimical* stare might...

3. It was *incumbent* on the team...

Exercise V

Writing

Here is a writing prompt similar to the one you will find on the writing portion of the ACT.

Living beyond one's means has become a way of life in America, one in which the status quo would seem to suggest everyone needs to have a new car (and car payment), high speed Internet access, cable television, and the latest smart phone. Those who cannot pay cash for these luxuries charge them on credit cards with astronomical interest rates, rendering repayment of the debt nearly impossible.

People who have substantial consumer debt have made themselves slaves for a few trivial comforts, trophies, or novelties. Some simply try to walk away from the debt they racked up, declaring bankruptcy and leaving their bills unpaid after having already enjoyed the pleasures they never paid for. Others pay debt using borrowed money, digging the hole yet deeper.

Certainly, debt is nothing anyone wants, but it is often necessary; few people, for example, have enough cash to purchase a house (though it's a great idea). What is your opinion of debt? What is acceptable debt, if there is such a thing, and what makes it acceptable? When is it OK to borrow money? When is borrowing money a poor idea?

As the new writer for your local newspaper's advice column, address the question of when it is wise to incur debt. Create at least one example situation to support your argument. Be sure that you take a position on when, or if, there is a good time to borrow money.

Thesis: Write a one-sentence response to the above assignment. Make certain this sentence offers a clear statement of your position.

Example: Borrowing money is only acceptable if it is needed to survive, and no more should be borrowed than is absolutely necessary.

_____

_____

Organizational Plan: If your thesis is the point on which you want to end, where does your essay need to begin? List the points of development that are inevitable in leading your reader from your beginning point to your end point. This list is your outline.

1. _____

2. _____

3. _____

Draft: Use your thesis as both your beginning and your end. Following your outline, write a good first draft of your essay. Remember to support all of your points with examples, facts, references to reading, etc.

Review and revise: Exchange essays with a classmate. Using the scoring guide for Word Choice on page 244, score your partner's essay (while he or she scores yours). Focus on word choice and the use of language conventions. If necessary, rewrite your essay to improve the word choice and use of language.

Exercise VI

English Practice

Improving Paragraphs
Read the following passage and then choose the best revision for the underlined portions of the paragraph. The questions will require you to make decisions regarding the revision of the reading selection. Some revisions are not of actual mistakes, but will improve the clarity of the writing.

[1]

(1) Have you ever driven down the road, seemingly at ease, perhaps exceeding the speed limit to arrive at your destination a bit more quickly? (2) Then, you <u>see a long line of cars waiting in line to pay</u>[1] the toll and realize that you now have to join them and become one of the poor idiots wasting time and costly gasoline. (3) People have engaged in this meaningless exercise ever since toll roads and toll bridges were invented. (4) Stop, go a few <u>feet, break, stop</u>[2] again, and then repeat the process more times than you can count as cars jostle for better positions like basketball players near the hoop. (5) <u>Drivers nervously dig</u>[3] in ashtrays and between car seats, fumbling for the correct change, dropping coins on the ground or attempting to back up their cars scrape the side of the tollbooth, leaving paint chips and chipped concrete as permanent marks of futility. (6) Sometimes you're in line for ten minutes or more before you reach the toll-taker and surrender your quarter, dollar, or life savings for the privilege of being on a <u>supposedly-fast</u>[4] route home.

1. A. NO CHANGE
   B. a long line of cars' waiting in line to pay
   C. a long line of cars waiting to pay
   D. a long line of cars, waiting, to pay

2. F. NO CHANGE
   G. feet, break and stop
   H. feet, brake, stop,
   J. feet, brake, stop

3. A. NO CHANGE
   B. Drivers are nervously digging
   C. Drivers dig nervously
   D. Digging nervously, drivers

4. F. NO CHANGE
   G. supposed-fast
   H. supposedly fast
   J. supposedly, fast

[2]

(7) Modern technology has finally given drivers the means of escaping the horrors of paying tolls <u>by having to stop their cars and then give the money to the tollbooth operator by hand</u>.[5] (8) New microchip transmitters affixed to windshields can be read by machines above the tollbooths, and the charges are billed automatically to drivers' credit cards. (9) This easy process requires drivers to register their cars, set up accounts, and pay the bill, that's all there is to it, it's as simple as that. (10) The driver can pass through the toll lane without stopping, while the fools in the pay-by-cash lane <u>wait his turns</u>.[6]

5. The redundancy of sentence 7 can be eliminated by
   A. replacing *give the money* with *pay.*
   B. starting a new sentence after *horrors.*
   C. referring to the information discussed in paragraph 1.
   D. replacing the underlined portion with *by hand.*

7. To correct an error in sentence 9, an editor would need to
   A. make all the verbs in the series infinitives.
   B. place a semicolon after *bill.*
   C. fix the comma splice by creating a new sentence between *it* and *its.*
   D. punctuate the three independent clauses properly.

6. F. NO CHANGE
   G. wait her turn
   H. wait their turn
   J. wait their turns

[3]

(11) The rewards of using the simple, plastic stick-ons are <u>enormous; drivers</u>[8] save time, gas, and wear and tear on their cars; some states, offer discounts to those who use the devices; pollution decreases; <u>fewer accidents</u>[9] occur; and there's no worrying about having enough cash for the toll.

8. F. NO CHANGE
   G. enormous: drivers
   H. enormous, and drivers
   J. enormous: because drivers

9. A. NO CHANGE
   B. less car accidents
   C. less accidents
   D. fewer car accidents

[4]

(12) Few things in life compare to the thrill of watching other drivers suffer the wrenching pain of losing time waiting in long lines—even such joys as graduation, finding money on the ground, getting a bike for Christmas, and falling in love. (13) It is this great pleasure in observing someone elses misfortune that separates us from the animals—not our ability to reason or use tools. (14) Humans love to gloat! (15) My own toll transmitter will arrive in the mail next week, and I'll then be able to enjoy the pleasure of smoothly gliding through booth after booth without having to stop.

10. Which choice corrects a grammatical error in sentence 13?
    F. Replace *us* with *them*.
    G. Replace *elses* with *else's*.
    H. Create an antecedent for *else*.
    J. Make *use tools* parallel with *to reason*.

[5]

(16) So, if you're in the <u>long line waiting to move an inch at a time</u>[11] for an hour because you're not intelligent enough to join the modern world, wave to me as I glide on by, because I'll be looking over at you with a smile on my face and a transmitter on my windshield.

11. A. NO CHANGE
    B. long line, waiting to move an inch at a time
    C. long line waiting to move and inch-at-a-time
    D. long line waiting to move forward at one inch a time

[6]

(17) Some paranoid people think this new use of electronic gadgetry is just another diabolical invention of the government for tracking citizens, so that it knows where we are, where we go, <u>the things that we are buying</u>,[12] and what we do. (18) That form of reasoning is illogical and false. (19) If the government wants to follow people's whereabouts, there are already plenty of ways to do so, like security cameras, Internet data gathering, bank reports, passport information, credit card statements, social security numbers, taxes, cell phone monitoring, etc. (20) One more intrusion into our personal lives will not make any difference at all. (21) To those people who refuse to get these electronic passes, I say, <u>if you don't have anything to hide, why worry?</u>[13]

12. F. NO CHANGE
    G. our buying of things
    H. what we buy
    J. buying that we do

13. A. NO CHANGE
    B. "if you don't have anything to hide, why worry?"
    C. "if you don't have anything to hide, why worry"?
    D. "If you don't have anything to hide, why worry?"

14. Which of the following revisions would improve the chronology of the passage?
    F. Exchange paragraphs 1 and 2.
    G. Exchange paragraphs 2 and 3.
    H. Exchange paragraphs 3 and 4.
    J. Exchange paragraphs 5 and 6.

15. If one paragraph must be removed from the passage, the best choice would be
    A. paragraph 1; an introduction is not necessary.
    B. paragraph 3; it does not support the topic of the passage.
    C. paragraph 4; it digresses into personal philosophy.
    D. paragraph 6; it challenges the topic of the passage.

REVIEW
Lessons 1–7

Exercise I

Sentence Completion

Choose the best pair of words to complete the sentence. Most choices will fit grammatically and will even make sense logically, but you must choose the pair that best fits the idea of the sentence.

1. Desperate to be acknowledged by the master artist, the _____ apprentices issued pious _____ in praise of the master's latest creation.
   A. archaic, maxims
   B. stygian, litanies
   C. churlish, anomalies
   D. servile, platitudes
   E. staid, moratoriums

2. The local villager spoke in such a heavily accented _____ that it sounded like _____ to the visitors, even though they spoke the same language.
   A. vernacular, gibberish
   B. flippancy, zealous
   C. kudos, sectarian
   D. axiom, vitriolic
   E. anecdotes, incantation

3. Insane with power, the tyrant _____ the belief that he was infallable; very quickly giant photographs and paintings of him became _____.
   A. expiated, efficacious
   B. revered, replete
   C. promulgated, ubiquitous
   D. convoluted, arable
   E. estranged, incumbent

4. The _____ spacecraft, buried amid the bones of long-extinct reptiles, did not frighten the archaeologist as much as the fact that the spacecraft had visible _____ on the hull—in English.
   A. antediluvian, nomenclature
   B. inimical, talisman
   C. cosmopolitan, coterie
   D. sanctimonious, nexus
   E. pellucid, compendium

5. Using convincing _____ and a few outright lies, the con artist _____ upon the government three freighters filled with obsolete weaponry and unserviceable ammunition.
   A. plethora, usurped
   B. litany, entreated
   C. scullions, expurgated
   D. camaraderie, vacillated
   E. sophistry, foisted

6. The _____ drill sergeant became _____ and screamed at Private Pyle, who thought no one would notice the candy bars he had stashed in his body armor before the combat exercise began.
   A. haughty, incumbent
   B. archaic, replete
   C. rife, arable
   D. procrustean, livid
   E. inimical, internecine

7. Many people believed the _____ about the movie stars, even though the story was nothing more than a(n) _____ urban legend, most likely untrue.
   A. axiom, coeval
   B. anecdote, apocryphal
   C. litany, frangible
   D. donnybrook, incongruous
   E. imbroglio, intrinsic

8. Elizabeth would rather own a plain, _____ car that gets her from point A to point B than have to make payments on an expensive luxury sedan that merely creates an illusion of her living a(n) _____ lifestyle.
   A. churlish, innocuous
   B. dulcet, interminable
   C. quotidian, sybaritic
   D. sectarian, efficacious
   E. procrustean, abstemious

Exercise II

Crossword Puzzle

Use the clues to complete the crossword puzzle. The answers consist of vocabulary words from lessons 1 through 7.

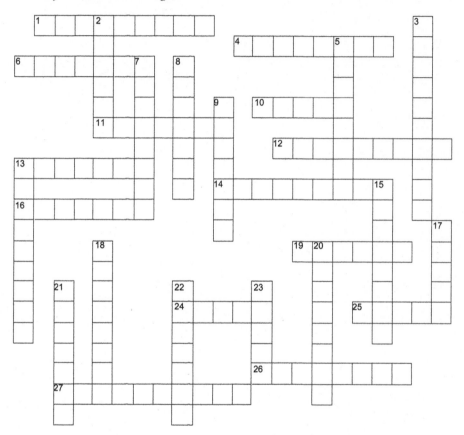

Across
1. release of emotional tension
4. clear
6. laughable
10. pass off as genuine
11. submissive
12. to waver
13. dark and forbidding
14. obligatory
16. full
19. dull recital
24. link
25. showing dignity
26. an overabundance
27. indifferent

Down
2. overbearing pride
3. occurring everywhere
5. plan cleverly
7. alienate
8. make amends for
9. trace of something
13. restrictive
15. shorten
17. shocking
18. servant
20. evil act
21. robber
22. odd occurrence
23. seize power

Vocabulary
Power Plus
for the **ACT**
Vocabulary,
Reading, and Writing
Exercises for High Scores

Lesson Eight

1. **pander** (pan´ dər) *v.* to exploit weaknesses of others; to cater to the vices of others
The trendy clothing store *pandered* to materialistic clients by selling shoddy clothing at outrageously high prices.
syn: cajole; indulge

2. **otiose** (ō´ shē ōs) *adj.* useless; futile
The director decided to remove the *otiose* scenes that increased the length of the film but failed to add to the suspense.
syn: unimportant; worthless   *ant: productive; necessary*

3. **puerile** (pyu´ ər əl) *adj.* childish; juvenile
Uncle Joe refused to tolerate his teenage nephew's *puerile* behavior.
syn: immature; infantile   *ant: mature*

4. **aleatory** (ā´ lē ə tôr ē) *adj.* dependent on luck or chance
Because of the uncertain weather forecast, the success of our company picnic is purely *aleatory*.

5. **asperity** (a sper´ i tē) *n.* roughness or harshness; severity
The teacher felt bad after his *asperity* caused a student to cry.
syn: acerbity; irascibility   *ant: mildness; kindness*

6. **renunciation** (ri nun sē ā´ shən) *n.* rejection; refusal to acknowledge
Members of the club responded to Bill's *renunciation* of their doctrine by asking him to leave.
syn: denial; refusal   *ant: admittance; concession*

7. **unimpeachable** (un im pē´ chə bəl) *adj.* unquestionable; beyond doubt
The Internet is not an *unimpeachable* source of information for academic research.
syn: trustworthy; infallible   *ant: questionable; flawed*

8. **inveigh** (in vā´) *v.* to disapprove angrily; to protest
Irene *inveighed* against her company's hiring of a former competitor for a prominent position.
syn: berate; condemn; remonstrate   *ant: commend; laud; praise*

9. **lionize** (lī′ ə nīz) *v.* to assign great social importance to; to treat as a celebrity
The public *lionized* the boy for saving the child from the burning building.
syn: acclaim; exalt; honor   *ant: ignore; overlook*

10. **allay** (ə lā′) *v.* to relieve; to alleviate
Mom tried to *allay* my fear of flying by reading favorable airline statistics.
syn: calm; ease; pacify   *ant: excite; intensify; agitate*

11. **vitiate** (vish′ ē āt) *v.* to corrupt morally; to contaminate
Mark claims that prisons simply *vitiate* the spirits of the inmates.
syn: defile; devalue; spoil   *ant: purify; clarify; cleanse*

12. **recalcitrant** (ri kal′ si trənt) *adj.* stubbornly resistant; showing opposition
The *recalcitrant* child kicked and screamed when the barber tried to give him his first haircut.
syn: defiant; insubordinate; unwilling   *ant: agreeable; obedient*

13. **exegesis** (ek sə jē′ sis) *n.* an explanation of a text; a critical interpretation
The students read an *exegesis* of *Macbeth* to understand the play better.
syn: analysis; exposition; commentary

14. **ameliorate** (ə mēl′ yə rāt) *v.* to make better; to improve
The manager asked for suggestions that might *ameliorate* working conditions at the factory.
syn: enhance; upgrade   *ant: weaken; damage; corrupt*

15. **profligate** (prof′ li git) *adj.* wasteful and immoral
The young heir lived a *profligate* life of alcohol, excess, and greed.
syn: licentious; decadent   *ant: virtuous; principled*

Exercise I

Words in Context

From the list below, supply the words needed to complete the paragraph. Some words will not be used.

unimpeachable	exegesis	otiose	renunciation
puerile	pander	recalcitrant	

1.   The defense attorney's _____ efforts to win the trial simply delayed the inevitable; the _____ evidence had quickly convinced the jury that the defendant was guilty. When the verdict was read, the defendant, a former executive, shocked courtroom observers with _____ remarks. Bailiffs then dragged the _____ prisoner from the courtroom, while he kicked and clawed at any court official within reach.

   "The defendant's blatant disregard for the law implies a complete _____ of it," said the judge, "demands a strict reprisal, which will be determined at the sentencing hearing tomorrow."

From the list below, supply the words needed to complete the paragraph. Some words will not be used.

aleatory	ameliorate	profligate	exegesis
inveigh	otiose	asperity	

2.   Tina liked her new first-floor apartment, but she couldn't stand the _____ upstairs tenants, who partied incessantly though the night, keeping everyone awake. After enduring several days of nonstop music and stomping, Tina visited the noisy neighbor and spoke with a[n] _____ she usually reserved for dealing with the most difficult of people.

   "You shouldn't require a[n] _____ of the lease to know that it's not proper to disturb every tenant in the building with your noise!" screamed Tina, in order to be heard over the blaring stereo. The offending neighbor simply closed the door, leaving Tina standing in the hall alone. During the week that followed, Tina encouraged her other neighbors to call the landlord and _____ against the habits of the noisy tenants so as to _____ the living conditions of the apartment building.

From the list below, supply the words needed to complete the paragraph. Some words will not be used.

pander   lionize   unimpeachable   aleatory
vitiate   allay   asperity

3.   The world of pop culture _____ the talk-radio host for his racy programs, but thousands of angry listeners claimed that his low humor and poorly supported arguments simply _____ his younger generations of listeners. The host, they claimed, _____ to the young by supplying their vivid imaginations with scenarios that defy traditional morality. Raising children properly is _____ enough, they argued, without adding counterproductive distractions. Network executives held a meeting, and in the following week, the network attempted to _____ the angry listeners' concerns by rescheduling the show to a late-night slot.

Exercise II

Sentence Completion

Complete the sentence in a way that shows you understand the meaning of the italicized vocabulary word.

1. Dan's *otiose* attempt to ski resulted in...

2. Ryan read an *exegesis* of the cryptic poem because...

3. Some citizens feared that the new casino would *vitiate*...

4. The man *pandered* to concert fans by selling T-shirts for twenty dollars each, even though he...

5. The *profligate* senator was voted out shortly after...

6. Teresa *inveighed* against the proposed landfill because...

7. Ted thought that firing more people would *ameliorate* the company's finances, but instead...

8. The criminal mistakenly thought that the public would *lionize* him if he...

9. The professor expected *puerile* comments from four-year-olds, but not...

10. It took three hours to convince the *recalcitrant*...

11. The inmate failed to convince the parole board of his complete *renunciation* of...

12. Harvey had an *unimpeachable* belief in ghosts after...

13. To *allay* the pain of your headache, you might...

14. The drill sergeant claimed that her *asperity* was necessary because it...

15. The baseball player made an *aleatory* promise to the sick youngster that he would...

Exercise III

Roots, Prefixes, and Suffixes

Study the entries and answer the questions that follow.

The roots *nat* and *nasc* mean "to be born."
The root *viv* means "to live."
The root *mort* means "to die."
The prefix *con* means "together."
The prefix *pre* means "before."
The suffix *fy* means "to make."

1. *Using literal translations as guidance, define the following words without using a dictionary.*

   A. mortify   D. nascent
   B. convivial E. vivify
   C. prenatal   F. vivid

2. A person born in a country is _____ to that country.

3. The root *sect* means "to cut apart"; *vivisection*, therefore, literally means
   _____.

4. What does a *mortician* do for a living?

5. List as many words as you can think of that contain the root *viv*.

Exercise IV

Inference

Complete the sentences by inferring information about the italicized word from its context.

1. Your motives must be *unimpeachable* if you plan to attempt something that...

2. Someone might *inveigh* against your plan if...

3. A *recalcitrant* child might refuse to...

Exercise V

Critical Reading

Below is a reading passage followed by several multiple-choice questions similar to the ones you will encounter on the ACT. Carefully read the passage and choose the best answer for each of the questions.

The author of the following passage comments on the significance of the Internet.

From protecting American lives to enriching the lives of people all over the world, the Internet stands as one of the greatest collaborative inventions of all time. In 1969, the Pentagon sponsored a network of computers at four major universities, creating a system that allowed the United States military to communicate and
5   maintain control over missiles during a simulated nuclear war. Researchers named the network ARPANET after the Advanced Research Projects Agency, a military technological think-tank. By the early seventies, thirty-seven computers communicated with each other via ARPANET. Ironically, what began as an effort to control the chaos of a nuclear holocaust soon morphed into a chaotic world of its
10 own.

Beginning in 1972 with the invention of electronic mail, ARPANET also functioned as a high-speed post office. At the First International Conference on Computers and Communication held in Washington, D.C., demonstrations of the network in action stimulated interest and research, and soon many more networks
15 appeared. In 1974, researchers began using a common language, Transmission Control Protocol and Internet Protocol (TCP/IP), that allowed the networks to communicate with each other. Stanford University researchers introduced a commercial version of ARPANET that same year, and they officially dubbed the ever-expanding network, the "Internet." In the years since, schools, libraries,
20 hospitals, and corporations hurried to connect to the Net; thus, the Internet revolutionized society's way of learning and sharing information.

Today, the Information Superhighway entices everyone to cruise its main drags and back roads; computer companies and Internet service providers boast incredible features at affordable prices, making it easier than ever to merge into the fast lane.
25 Combined with incredible video technology, the Internet offers casual users a scenic route for their information road trip, on which they can enjoy the picturesque view of vacation spots, pictures from the grandchildren, or the photographic evidence that the perfect chocolate cake recipe really does exist. Educators and their students use the Internet's myriad news and reference sites to access valuable information.
30 Scientists use the Internet more than ever, communicating text, pictures, and movie footage with peers all over the world. Medical professionals exchange life-saving information with each other, and post that information for patient access. Gone are the days when the Internet belonged solely to military scientists and university researchers.

35   Despite its obvious benefits, the Internet is not without its criticism, some of which contends that the Internet is doomed to implode as independent, intelligent thought disappears in a nuclear mushroom cloud of muddled misinformation and relationships, causing community to cease altogether.

    Since the rise of the Internet, people no longer use libraries, encyclopedias,
40 or their own brains to solve problems. When boredom strikes and an original idea does not, people surf the sea of mediocrity known as the World Wide Web, accepting as truth everything they see there. They dismiss their powers of logic and common sense in favor of following blindly the simulacrum-strewn path of Internet misinformation. Thus, overuse and abuse of the Internet promotes banality of
45 thought, slovenliness of research habits, and sheer idiocy of behavior.

    The Internet hampers an entire generation's ability to focus by constantly interrupting it with pop-up advertisements and instant messages begging for response, pandering to youthful cravings for instant gratification. Furthermore, the Internet promotes hate, and hate unchecked decimates faster than the Black Death.
50 Prejudice prevails thanks to a plethora of propaganda-based websites espousing ethnic and cultural superiority. Even the most ignorant cretin can post on any number of Internet locations with malicious intent and simultaneous impunity. Hatemongers remain anonymous by using screen names, web pseudonyms that cannot be traced; thus, these insolent Internet users participate in on-line anarchy,
55 avoiding censorship, regulation, and accountability.

    Like dynamite or atomic energy, the Internet's great potential for good is equaled only by its potential for bad. The Internet is a tool for personal excellence as much as it is a virtual altar at which millions of sex addicts faithfully worship. Over 300 million pages of pornography clog the web, many of which exploits the
60 poor, the homeless, or the substance co-addicted.

    In addition to causing moral decay, time online (regardless of the activity pursued) also leads to isolationism and the deterioration of social relationships. Who needs to visit friends when an e-mail will suffice? Who needs to attend religious services when groups can worship online? Virtual communities fill the
65 emptiness with pseudo-socialization that requires no commitment, laying waste to real families and real neighborhoods. Lazy consumers no longer need to leave the house to shop. Slacking singles can go on virtual dates that require no preparation. Uninformed patients can visit web doctors for dubious professional opinions, sight unseen. Soon, a generation of children with bold, gregarious chat room
70 personalities will refuse to leave their own homes because they might be required— it's frightening—to speak to an actual stranger in person.

    Balance, then, and vigilance must be applied to the superhighway of information. Generations yet to come can become victim to Internet-induced agoraphobia, reduced to a collective of pale, atrophied, hermits who buy groceries, get educated,
75 get married and have children online, or they can separate the wheat from the chaff and become the most enlightened, connected civilization in the history of Earth. We'll see how it goes.

1. According to the passage, researchers developed the Internet to
    A. enrich lives through enhanced communication.
    B. send e-mail from universities to military bases.
    C. provide a cheap means of intercollegiate communication.
    D. maintain control of weapons after a nuclear attack.

2. In paragraph 3, the author uses a metaphor to
    F. foreshadow the expansion of the Internet.
    G. compare the Internet to a highway.
    H. add humor to the passage.
    J. explain how language changes to reflect technology.

3. Lines 35-38 do not include which one of the following:
    A. two antithetical remarks
    B. a reference to an actual nuclear war
    C. instances of alliteration
    D. a simile comparing intelligence and incorrect information

4. Which of the following best describes the tone of the passage?
    F. optimistic but cautious
    G. comical and humorous
    H. critical and judgmental
    J. technical and authoritative

5. In line 45, the word *sheer* most nearly means
    A. transparent.
    B. to slice.
    C. unmitigated.
    D. very steep.

6. In line 51, the word *cretin* most nearly means
    F. innocent person.
    G. idiotic person.
    H. unconcerned person.
    J. silly person.

7. Beginning with line 50, the author uses a series of words that begin with the same sounds. The author uses this alliteration in order to
   A. make the paragraph read like a poem.
   B. impart an encoded message to readers.
   C. demonstrate the language of anonymous chat rooms.
   D. emphasize the condemning tone of the paragraph.

8. Which statement best summarizes the implication of lines 61-71?
   F. Most people reject online relationships.
   G. Gamers are most prone to Internet addiction.
   H. Moral decay will cause decay of individuality and original thought.
   J. Users will opt for pseudo-interaction before real, physical, social interaction.

9. The author of the passage would probably agree that
   A. the Internet should be abolished.
   B. the military gave the private sector the impetus for the Internet.
   C. the Internet should be celebrated.
   D. the Internet has a bright future.

10. Which of the following does not describe one of the threats of the Internet as portrayed in the passage?
    F. suppression of original thought
    G. greed of Internet commerce revenue
    H. moral decay and decline
    J. timid, ineffective personalities

Vocabulary
Power Plus
for the ACT
Vocabulary,
Reading, and Writing
Exercises for High Scores

Lesson Nine

1. **provocative** (prə vok´ ə tiv) *adj.* tending to excite or stimulate
    The daughter considered her mother's short skirt too *provocative*.
    syn: provoking; exciting   *ant: dull; boring*

2. **bumpkin** (bump´ kin) *n.* an unsophisticated, awkward person
    Pickpockets often prey on *bumpkins* who forget to protect their wallets
    while visiting the city.
    syn: yokel; hayseed; rube   *ant: intellectual*

3. **toady** (tō´ dē) *n.* a person who flatters for personal gain
    The *toady* followed the young queen around, agreeing with every idiotic
    statement she uttered.
    syn: sycophant; flatterer

4. **culpable** (kul´ pə bəl) *adj.* deserving blame or condemnation; guilty
    The prosecutor said that the crime boss was *culpable* for the murders
    even though he himself did not kill the victims.
    syn: blameworthy; liable   *ant: innocent; blameless*

5. **hortatory** (hor´ tə tōr ē) *adj.* encouraging; inciting
    The troops cheered during the general's *hortatory* speech.
    syn: exhorting   *ant: discouraging; dampening*

6. **penultimate** (pi nəl´ tə mət) *adj.* next to last
    The *penultimate* step before graduation will be passing my final
    examinations.

7. **orotund** (ôr´ ə tund) *adj.* full and rich in sound (in speech)
    The narrator of the movie advertisement spoke in a deep, *orotund* voice.
    syn: resonant; resounding   *ant: quiet; reserved*

8. **blithe** (blīth) *adj.* carefree and lighthearted
    The sight of his childhood home caused Jerry to reminisce about his *blithe*
    days of picking blueberries and fishing in the creek behind the house.
    syn: cheerful; radiant   *ant: burdened; worried; troubled*

9. **soporific** (sop ə rif´ ik) *adj.* tending to induce sleep
   I stopped reading the *soporific* novel and found a more exciting one.
   syn: somniferous; monotonous   *ant: dramatic; exciting;*
   stimulating

10. **pervasive** (pər vā´ siv) *adj.* permeating; spreading throughout
    In two days, everyone in the small town had heard the *pervasive* rumor.
    syn: sweeping; persistent   *ant: contained; restricted; limited*

11. **benign** (bi nīn´) *adj.* beneficial; favorable
    She let down her guard when she saw his *benign* expression.
    syn: benevolent; harmless   *ant: harmful; malevolent*

12. **frenetic** (frə net´ ik) *adj.* wildly excited
    The neighbors heard the *frenetic* barks of the dog that fell into the well.
    syn: frenzied; frantic   *ant: calm; composed*

13. **recrimination** (ri krim ə nā´ shən) *n.* a counteraccusation
    The burglar had the nerve to express *recriminations* against the
    homeowner for hitting him with a shovel.
    syn: countercharge

14. **indecorous** (in dek´ ər əs) *adj.* lacking good taste; improper
    The heckler made *indecorous* comments during the candidate's speech.
    syn: inappropriate; vulgar   *ant: decent*

15. **corroborate** (kə rob´ ə rāt) *v.* to strengthen by adding evidence
    The doctor's note *corroborated* Bill's excuse for missing a week of work.
    syn: confirm; substantiate; validate   *ant: contradict*

Exercise I

Words in Context

From the list below, supply the words needed to complete the paragraph. Some words will not be used.

benign	soporific	indecorous	bumpkin
pervasive	corroborate	frenetic	

1. David loved to spend time with his grandparents, but he loathed the
    _____ drive through three hundred miles of midwestern cornfields.
    Halfway through the trip, Dave pulled over at a dusty little gas station for
    coffee and fuel. Two _____ clad in bib overalls sat in lawn chairs near
    the front door, staring at Dave—they didn't often see city folk at their tiny
    outpost. He gave a[n] _____ nod to them before placing the pump
    nozzle into his fuel tank; he didn't want to be _____ during his first
    visit to the country in years. As the ancient pump made audible "dings" to
    mark each gallon of gas, Dave stepped away from the car and breathed in
    the _____ smell of corn husks.

From the list below, supply the words needed to complete the paragraph. Some words will not be used.

frenetic	orotund	provocative	pervasive
toady	hortatory	culpable	

2. The successful novelist knew that her latest book, a[n] _____
    tale of star-crossed lovers and murder-for-hire, was not her best, but her
    agent, a fawning _____ who simply wanted more money and fame,
    said it was her best writing to date. Anne knew better than to take her
    agent's _____ comments seriously; he was simply _____ about
    receiving his guaranteed dividend as stated in the contract. Anne was the
    one who was _____ in imparting sudden, undeserved wealth to her
    agent; she had prematurely signed a six-year contract before she realized
    that she didn't need an agent to sell her books in the first place.

From the list below, supply the words needed to complete the paragraph. Some words will not be used.

recrimination	blithe	toady	orotund
corroborate	bumpkin	penultimate	

3.   A[n] _____ group of children abandoned their game of marbles to flock around the burly man delivering a[n] _____ sales pitch from the top of a wagon in the town square. He was selling genuine musical instruments, he said, and he _____ his claims by unveiling samples of trumpets, clarinets, flutes, and even some snare drums. In response to those in the crowd who asserted that he was simply a scam artist who would take everyone's money and leave town without providing the instruments, the quick-witted man expressed overly forceful _____, suggesting that his accusers simply feared that the town's children might have an opportunity that their parents never had. In three days, the salesman had collected enough orders—and cash—to complete the _____ step in his plan: to get as far away from the little town as he possibly could before the people realized that they had been conned.

Exercise II

Sentence Completion

Complete the sentence in a way that shows you understand the meaning of the italicized vocabulary word.

1.   The child's mother's *frenetic* shouts became…

2.   No single person is *culpable* for…

3.   Fans came from all around to hear the *orotund* voice of…

4.   The sound of the ocean had a *soporific* effect that caused…

5.   It was once considered *provocative* for people to show affection in public, but now…

6.   Without realizing the danger, the poorly informed *bumpkin* walked right into…

7.   Talking on a cellular phone is *indecorous* behavior when you are…

8.   For many people, the *penultimate* step before going to sleep at night is to…

9. Charles looked forward to the *blithe* days he'd have during…

10. The wealthy broker grew tired of *toadies* who…

11. Victor said that *recriminations* against…

12. The villagers grabbed their pitchforks and torches after the mayor's *hortatory* rallying cries to…

13. Unless you can *corroborate* your need for additional funding, the government will…

14. During our trek through the desert, the *pervasive* dust and sand…

15. When the doctor explained that the growth was *benign*, the patient…

Exercise III

Roots, Prefixes, and Suffixes

Study the entries and answer the questions that follow.

The root *spir* means "to breathe."
The root *hal* means "to breathe."
The root *neur* means "nerve."
The prefix *con* means "together."
The prefix *ex* means "out."
The prefix *a* means "towards."
The suffix *osis* means "sickness," "condition," or "process."

1. *Using literal translations as guidance, define the following words without using a dictionary.*

    A. exhalation   D. halitosis
    B. conspire   E. aspire
    C. expire   F. neurosis

2. If you are said to have _____, then you are full of energy, or the "breath of life."

3. A device that helps asthma sufferers breathe is called a(n) _____.

4. If *per* means "through," then *perspire* literally means _____.

5. List as many words as you can think of that contain the prefix *ex*.

Exercise IV

Inference

Complete the sentences by inferring information about the italicized word from its context.

1. If no one can *corroborate* your story that you were home on the night of the burglary, the court might...

2. The inspectors at the factory will need to find the person *culpable* for the tragic explosion so they can...

3. On the school bus, the children's *frenetic* behavior caused...

Exercise V

Writing

Here is a writing prompt similar to the one you will find on the writing portion of the ACT.

It has been said that the only thing necessary for the triumph of evil is for good people to do nothing. Indeed, few things are more horrifying than news footage of bystanders witnessing a crime, an assault, or a person in medical distress, and doing nothing to intervene. Like sheep, people simply watch, perhaps wide-eyed as they fumble with cell phones, or else they keep walking with eyes averted, afraid, seemingly, to intervene in the business of others. There is even a name for this repulsive behavior: the bystander effect. In many situations, especially those in which embarrassment might be a consequence of intervening, quiet, cowardly avoidance overpowers the human sense of duty to his or her fellow humans.

Sadly, the bystander effect manifests itself in all facets of life and has contributed to many of the events now regarded as horrors and catastrophes in human history. Tragedies might occur slowly, as residents of a small town watch poisons get dumped into their aquifer for decades, for example, or they might occur at a national level in the form of a specific ethnic group's being blamed and persecuted as the cause of a nation's financial failures. When no one challenges injustices, tragedies occur.

What must be done to help people overcome the bystander effect? Think of activities, exercises, or education that will galvanize people into taking action on behalf of others. You might have an idea for classes, training, camps, or even a convincing story. Detail your solution in a letter to a newspaper and explain the necessity of your program.

Thesis: Write a one-sentence response to the above assignment. Make certain this sentence offers a clear statement of your position.

Example: The first step in getting people to serve others in need is to get them to imagine themselves in situations in which they are in need.

_____

_____

Organizational Plan: If your thesis is the point on which you want to end, where does your essay need to begin? List the points of development that are inevitable in leading your reader from your beginning point to your end point. This list is your outline.

1. _____

2. _____

3. _____

Draft: Use your thesis as both your beginning and your end. Following your outline, write a good first draft of your essay. Remember to support all of your points with examples, facts, references to reading, etc.

Review and revise: Exchange essays with a classmate. Using the Holistic scoring guide on page 245, score your partner's essay (while he or she scores yours). If necessary, rewrite your essay to correct the problems indicated by the essay's score.

Exercise VI

English Practice

Identifying Sentence Errors

Identify the errors in the following sentences. Choose the answer that fixes the error. If the sentence contains no error, select NO CHANGE.

1. <u>However hard</u> it rains, the frogs in my pond continue to enjoy themselves; when the weather changes, though, they begin to prepare for hibernation.
   A. NO CHANGE
   B. How ever hard
   C. However, hardly
   D. However difficult

2. Betty, <u>whom had the best average of anyone else in math class</u>, could not believe her ears when the teacher said, "Betty, you must not have studied for this test; you missed half the answers."
   F. NO CHANGE
   G. whom had the best average of anyone in math class
   H. who had the best average in math class
   J. who had the highest average of anyone in class

3. The lost campers wandered through the mountains, camped each night wherever they could, ate wild berries, managed to avoid bears and mountain <u>lions and never</u> gave up hope.
   A. NO CHANGE
   B. lions, and never
   C. lions and, never,
   D. lions: and never

4. The little children chased the rabbits into burrows and didn't worry about anything, while the <u>kid's parents</u> worried about mosquitoes.
   F. NO CHANGE
   G. kid's parent's
   H. kids parent's
   J. kids' parents

5. Tiffany's new <u>car, that</u> requires high octane fuel, can really fly down the highway.
   A. NO CHANGE
   B. car that
   C. car, which
   D. car which

Improving Sentences

The underlined portion of each sentence below contains some flaw. Select the answer that best corrects the flaw.

6. During the hot, dry summer, commercial farmers growing fruits and grains in low elevations recognized <u>they needed more water to survive, they installed new irrigation systems.</u>

    F. that farmers needed more water to survive so they installed new irrigation systems.

    G. that the plants would not survive without more water; for that reason, the farmers installed new irrigation systems.

    H. they were going to lose the crops if no one installed new irrigation systems.

    J. they needed more water for the plants, and the plants would not survive so they, the farmers, installed new irrigation systems.

7. The family of doctors traces <u>their medical heritage back to the sixteen hundreds.</u>

    A. its medical heritage to the seventeenth century.

    B. their medical heritage back to the 1600s.

    C. their heritage back to the seventeenth century.

    D. its medical history back to the sixteenth century.

8. <u>Playing until one o'clock in the morning, the police were called</u> to shut down the concert.

    F. Playing until one o'clock in the morning, someone called the police

    G. Playing until 1:00 a.m., the police were called

    H. At one o'clock in the morning, the police were called

    J. By playing until one o'clock in the morning, the police were called

9. <u>Because the math problems were difficult for me to do, I had forgotten all the equations.</u>

    A. I had forgotten all the equations, because the math problems were difficult for me to complete.

    B. The math problems were difficult for me because I had forgotten to do all the equations.

    C. The math problems were difficult to do, but all the equations had been forgotten by me.

    D. The math problems were difficult to do because I had forgotten all the equations.

10. <u>After Mr. Edwards died, workers at his company realize how much he did for the neighborhood, and they have been circulating</u> a petition to have a street named after him.

    F. After Mr. Edwards died, workers at his company realized how much he had done for the neighborhood, and they have been circulating

    G. After Mr. Edwards died, workers at his company realized what he did for the neighborhood and since then they have circulated

    H. When Mr. Edwards died, workers at his company, realizing how much he does for the neighborhood, had been circulating

    J. Mr. Edwards died, and workers at his company realized how much he has done for the neighborhood, and since then they have been circulating

Vocabulary
Power Plus
for the **ACT**
Vocabulary,
Reading, and Writing
Exercises for High Scores

Lesson Ten

1. **majordomo** (mā jər-dō´ mō) *n.* a chief butler or assistant
   The baron's *majordomo* tends the estate while his master is away.

2. **untenable** (un ten´ ə bəl) *adj.* impossible to defend or justify
   The judge's dismissal of the defendant's *untenable* claim was due to lack
   of evidence.
   syn: groundless; unsupported; indefensible   *ant: sound; irrefutable*

3. **perambulate** (pə ram´ byə lāt) v. to walk about; to stroll
   Though arthritic, the elderly woman could still *perambulate* among the
   brilliantly flowered paths of her garden.
   syn: saunter; wander

4. **veneer** (və nēr´) *n.* a thin, attractive layer that conceals something
      common or coarse
   He disguised his greed with a *veneer* of smiles and charitable words.
   syn: disguise; gloss; facade

5. **timorous** (tim´ ər əs) *adj.* timid
   The puppy was so small and *timorous* that all its siblings bullied it.
   syn: bashful; sheepish; reticent   *ant: bold; confident; courageous*

6. **luminous** (lōō´ mə nəs) *adj.* emitting light
   That wristwatch has *luminous* numbers so you can see them at night.
   syn: glowing; radiant   *ant: dim; dark*

7. **circuitous** (sər kyōō´ i təs) *adj.* indirect; roundabout
   The bridge flooded the highway, so we were forced to take a *circuitous*
   detour that added two hours to our trip.
   syn: roundabout; meandering   *ant: direct; straight*

8. **perquisite** (pər´ kwə zət) *n.* a tip or payment in addition to regular wages
   The *perquisite* of a company car offset the job's mediocre salary.
   syn: fringe benefit; perk; benefit

9. **probity** (prō´ bə tē) *n.* integrity; respectability
   Though still a teenager, Irene had the *probity* to be a trustworthy babysitter.
   syn: rectitude; decency; trustworthiness   *ant: wickedness; impiety*

10. **polemical** (pə lə´ mi kəl) *adj.* relating to controversy or argument
    The mayor's *polemical* statement jeopardized his political career.
    syn: controversial; contentious   *ant: indisputable; agreeable*

11. **tacit** (tas´ it) *adj.* indicated but not expressed; implied silently
    Dad didn't want me to go to the concert, but he gave his *tacit* approval
    by saying nothing when I asked permission to go.
    syn: hinted; suggested; unspoken   *ant: explicit; frank*

12. **largesse** (lär zhes´) *n.* generosity
    Building the art center would have been impossible if it were not for the
    largesse of several wealthy benefactors.
    syn: magnanimity; munificence   *ant: stinginess*

13. **indolent** (in´ də lənt) *adj.* lazy
    The first round of firings removed *indolent* workers who looked as
    though they were not working.
    syn: idle; lethargic; torpid   *ant: industrious; busy; productive*

14. **circumlocution** (sûr kəm lō kyōō´ shən) *n.* unnecessarily wordy or
    evasive language
    When the teacher asked about her progress on the science project, the
    student's *circumlocution* revealed that she had not even begun it.
    syn: discursiveness; indirectness; evasion   *ant: conciseness; brevity*

15. **depredate** (dep ri dāt´) *v.* to plunder and pillage
    During the riot, revelers *depredated* the banks and museums.
    syn: pilfer; ransack; ravage   *ant: enhance*

Exercise I

Words in Context

From the list below, supply the words needed to complete the paragraph. Some words will not be used.

largesse	luminous	probity	majordomo
perquisite	circuitous	depredate	

1. The _____ that we associate with protective service workers, such as firemen, did not develop until the late twentieth century. Police, fire departments, and ambulance services have taken a[n] _____ route to becoming the professional organizations that we know today. Before fire departments were organized, victims relied upon the _____ of neighbors using bucket brigades to save their homes; however, sometimes that was a better option than requesting assistance from the fire department. In cities, looters among volunteer firemen sometimes _____ burning homes before the flames destroyed all the valuables and brought the buildings to the ground. If faced with fighting two fires simultaneously, fire brigades responded only to the blaze that would result in better _____ for their department. The other house was left to burn.

From the list below, supply the words needed to complete the paragraph. Some words will not be used.

depredate	polemical	circumlocution	timorous
majordomo	tacit	veneer	

2. No one had seen the reclusive billionaire, Mr. Tanket, for months. Most people saw only Tanket's _____, who had the legal authority to make decisions on Tanket's behalf. Even during a[n] _____ merger that resulted in thousands of layoffs, Mr. Tanket was not to be found. Some speculated that Tanket's hiding was a _____ clue that he had actually passed away and that the corporation was covering it up. When asked about it, representatives offered only _____ that changed the subject and failed to answer any questions. Soon, every investigative reporter in the nation was trying to chip through the _____ that might be concealing some dark secret of the corporation.

From the list below, supply the words needed to complete the paragraph. Some words will not be used.

untenable	perquisite	indolent	luminous
perambulate	timorous	veneer	

3.   Phillip knew that no one would believe his _____ story about seeing a bright, _____ object hovering over his cornfield. On the night of the sighting, Phillip tried to _____ through the field to get a closer look, but the tall cornstalks obscured his view of the object, which vanished as he neared it. Perhaps, thought Phillip, whoever was flying the object was too _____ to confront an Earthling. The other villagers heckled Phillip during breakfast at the diner on the following morning.

     "If you hadn't been so _____ and not harvested your crop on time," one farmer joked, "you would have been able to wave at your moon men."

Exercise II

Sentence Completion

Complete the sentence in a way that shows you understand the meaning of the italicized vocabulary word.

1. Hank worried that thieves might *depredate* his house while...

2. The *majordomo* didn't answer the door; that was the job of...

3. Shane thought that he deserved occasional *perquisites* because...

4. The town was grateful for the *largesse* of the widow when...

5. The coffee table is made of cheap fiberboard, but it has a *veneer* that...

6. The *circuitous* marathon required participants to...

7. Matt began a tedious *circumlocution* when...

8. Few people agreed with Doug's *untenable* reason for...

9. The candidate was forced to defend his own *probity* when his opponent...

10. When the red light on the camera becomes *luminous*, you will know that...

11. Sometimes, the *indolent* night watchman...

12. The angry prospector could not convince his mule to *perambulate* around...

13. The department chairperson gave her *tacit* permission to...

14. Please spare us your *polemical* remarks so that we can...

15. A *timorous* person would probably not...

Exercise III

Roots, Prefixes, and Suffixes

Study the entries and answer the questions that follow.

The roots *pel* and *puls* mean "push."
The root *vect* means "carry."
The root *port* means "carry."
The root *com* means "together" or "with."
The prefixes *in* and *im* mean "in" or "into."
The suffix *or* means "one who does."

1. *Using literal translations as guidance, define the following words without using a dictionary.*

    A. import   D. impel
    B. comport   E. invective
    C. convection   F   compel

2. A laboratory animal that is carrying a disease is called a[n] _____, but someone who carries your luggage in a hotel is called a[n] _____.

3. If you want to check the rate at which your heart is pushing blood throughout your body, you check your _____. A[n] _____ is a sudden feeling that pushes you to do something.

4. List as many words as you can think of that contain the root *port*.

Exercise IV

Inference

Complete the sentences by inferring information about the italicized word from its context.

1. If you can't speak for fear of being overheard, you might give someone a *tacit* message by...

2. Someone who cannot *perambulate* because of injuries to his or her legs might...

3. During a battle, soldiers might need to abandon an *untenable* position because...

Exercise V

Critical Reading

Below is a reading passage followed by several multiple-choice questions similar to the ones you will encounter on the ACT. Carefully read the passage and choose the best answer for each of the questions.

The following passage describes an incident involving a snake.

The day was warm and bright when I, as a teenager many years ago, walked down the camp road from the mess hall to the athletic field. A small crowd was gathering around a groundskeeper, and all the young campers were staring at the ground near the man's foot. As I approached, I heard amid the mumblings
5   of semi-concerned adolescents, "Snake!" and "Hey, there's a snake over here." Looking down, I saw the writhing mass of tensed coils nearly crushed beneath the maintenance man's boot. I had previously been bitten by scores of non-poisonous snakes, which didn't hurt a bit, so naturally, I had no fear of this particular one and reached toward it while telling the man to lift his foot slowly.
10   It took less than a second for the copperhead to strike and bite me twice on my left hand, directly on that tender portion between the thumb and forefinger known as the "snuff box." In the remainder of that second, the sting of self-consciousness made me blink dumbly, open-mouthed—that sting of embarrassment that often accompanies a feat of stupidity. I watched as a knot about the size of an egg
15   formed on my hand; this snake, now being ground into the gravel beneath Ed the groundskeeper's steel-toed boot, was definitely not a harmless reptile. I walked slowly to the camp infirmary, staring agape at the lump on my hand. Somehow, maybe from a flyer on the camp bulletin board, maybe from a past adventure comic book, I remembered that panic and rapid movement caused venom to circulate
20   more quickly, so I made it a point to overcome my instinct to run, screaming, with my arms flailing overhead.
      Luckily it was Wednesday, so Larry, the camp doctor, was in the infirmary lodge. He immersed my hand in hot water (which I later learned was the wrong thing to do), told me to stay still, and then he left for about twenty minutes while I
25   stood there listening to my heart thump faster with the thought of going blind, or convulsing, or whatever it was that this snake's venom was going to do to me. Larry returned with a scalpel, of all things, and the sunlight coming through the open doorway glinted off the blade in a warming way. The pain began in earnest now, and it was the start of the worst agony imaginable; I would later describe it as having my
30   hand in a red-hot vise. The doctor made four small incisions over the fang marks. I eventually found out that during the time Larry was gone, Ed, who had killed the snake, was looking in an encyclopedia to determine what kind of snake it was. The swelling crept slowly up my arm, and just seeing it made it hurt more. There was no antivenin available, so Larry called an ambulance to take me to a nearby hospital
35   where some could be administered. Now I panicked.

I started to cry from the indescribable pain. Sweat and fright oozed out of me, out of each pore. I couldn't believe that I was going to become one of those people I read about—that kid who died for being so stupid. I heard the ambulance's siren, which gave me an iota of hope, but oh, the ordeal was far from over, and there was
40 lots of suffering to be had.

I tried to walk to the door to see the ambula–and oh! I fainted, and what momentary bliss it was. Larry had lifted me from beneath my arms and began dragging me outside when I woke up again, and the pain had increased exponentially, as punishment for the temporary relief of unconsciousness. In the
45 ambulance, the serious look of the paramedic reminded me to panic, but not as much as his ordering the driver to "Step on it! This kid's in trouble!" During the fast ride, my swollen arm seemed to absorb the shock of every tiny bump that that steel-wheeled wagon of an ambulance ran over. After what felt like hours of torture, the rear doors flew open and the two paramedics shuffled me to gurney as I grunted
50 and howled simultaneously.

In the emergency room, through eyes welling with tears of pain, I caught a blurred glimpse of a grave-looking doctor holding what appeared to be some kind of gigantic, novelty syringe filled with yellow liquid. Before I had the chance to protest, he sank the needle into an arm so swollen that I didn't even recognize
55 it when I looked down. I yelped, choking on my own screams as the throbbing pain skyrocketed. "Stop it! Make it stop!" I moaned in agony, through clenched, grinding teeth. Then, through squinted eyes, I saw my mother, or so I thought, standing next to the gurney. "Don't worry," she said. Unfortunately, it didn't calm me or lessen the pain, so I continued to scream, my throat now getting hoarse. After
60 yet another interminable period of recoiling and howling, I was pinned down by the doctor long enough for him to inject some kind of painkiller, and finally, the pain subsided and I drifted off into a fitful sleep.

I woke up the next day—literally, the next day. I slept for twenty-four hours, and miraculously, the pain was gone. There were, however, a few after-effects.
65 When I looked down, I found an arm three times the diameter of the one that had been there the day before; it looked like a bodybuilder's arm, but it was impossible to bend it. My left hand looked ridiculous: it was twice its normal size, and it had three large blisters on it, each the size of a ping-pong ball. The swelling stretched the whole way to my neck. It took a week of physical therapy to get my arm
70 moving again.

My family had arrived during the night while I slept uneasily, and they told me that I had been critical for a long while. Later in the week, while I exercised my arm by tugging on a nylon bungee cord tied to the bed rail, Larry visited and brought me the snakeskin mounted on a board. It was an amazing forty-three inches long.
75 Now, many years after my learning experience, I still can't flatten my left hand. Perhaps when I figure out why I tried to grab that snake in the first place, I'll figure out how to move my hand again. Until that time, I'll just call Ed if I see a snake.

1. The main purpose of this passage is
   A. to warn people to avoid snakes.
   B. to explain medical procedures for a snakebite.
   C. to describe a personal memory.
   D. to demonstrate how youth believes itself to be invincible.

2. The overall tone or mood of this passage is best described as
   F. reflective.
   G. humorous.
   H. speculative.
   J. blameful.

3. Which choice best explains why the author included the following sentence?

   Larry returned with a scalpel, of all things, and the sunlight coming
   through the open doorway glinted off the blade in a warming way.

   A. The description foreshadows the trip to the hospital.
   B. The author is using irony to suggest the sight of the scalpel is frightening.
   C. The scalpel is a symbol of the author's rite of passage.
   D. The author is explaining why the doctor is described as insane.

4. The word *antivenin* in line 34 most nearly means
   F. some type of poison.
   G. medication for infection.
   H. strong tranquilizer.
   J. something to counteract poison.

5. In paragraph 3, what purpose does the disjointed time frame serve?
   A. It is unintentionally confusing.
   B. The paragraph is intended to show that the author is still alive.
   C. It is purposely jumbled to confuse the reader.
   D. It heightens the confusion of the actual incident.

6. According to the passage, the author has a hallucination in which
   F. he rides in a wagon.
   G. he sees a giant syringe.
   H. he picks up a poison snake.
   J. he sees his mother.

7. In paragraph 6, the word *interminable* most nearly means
    A. apparent.
    B. awkward.
    C. unending.
    D. regretful.

8. According to the passage, which is not one of the things that the author experienced?
    F. vomiting
    G. passing out
    H. swelling
    J. fear

9. This passage would probably be found in
    A. a book on snakes.
    B. a diary.
    C. a book report.
    D. an outdoor magazine.

10. Ed is
    F. the doctor.
    G. the groundskeeper.
    H. the paramedic.
    J. the kid who found the snake.

Vocabulary
Power Plus
for the **ACT**
Vocabulary,
Reading, and Writing
Exercises for High Scores

Lesson Eleven

1. **canard** (kə närd´) *n.* a deliberately misleading story
    The thief used the *canard* of his car's being broken down to lure victims
    into the alley.
    syn: lie; pretense; sham   *ant: fact; truth; reality*

2. **wont** (wont) *adj.* likely
    Be careful: that dog is *wont* to bite strangers.
    syn: accustomed

3. **etymology** (et ə mol´ ə jē) *n.* the history of a word; the study of word
        origins
    If you trace the *etymology* of the word "khaki," you will find that it
    comes from the Persian word for "dust."

4. **cortege** (kôr tezh´) *n.* a group of attendants; a retinue
    The royal *cortege* filled every room of a hotel floor during the queen's visit.
    syn: entourage; followers; posse

5. **solecism** (sä´ lə si zəm) *n.* a deviation or error in speech, manners, or deeds
    Using the word "less" instead of "fewer" when referring to individual
    items is a common *solecism*.
    syn: mistake; faux pas; blunder

6. **demotic** (di mot´ ik) *adj.* relating to ordinary people
    The nuclear physicist had trouble explaining his theories in *demotic* language.
    syn: colloquial; common   *ant: formal; elevated*

7. **simian** (si´ mē ən) *adj.* related to or resembling an ape or monkey
    The photograph of the alleged Bigfoot showed a *simian* creature walking
    upright through the forest.

8. **impresario** (im pri sär´ ē ō) *n.* an entertainment producer or manager
    The *impresario* of the concert hall had to book the famous soloist two
    years in advance.
    syn: organizer; proprietor

9. **requisite** (rek´ wi zit) *adj.* required; necessary
   Glenn's loan application was rejected because he omitted some *requisite* information.
   syn: imperative; needed; important   *ant: incidental; nonessential*

10. **bulwark** (bul´ wərk) *n.* a defensive wall or embankment
    Residents constructed a *bulwark* of sandbags to protect the town from the rising tide.
    syn: fortification; barrier

11. **malaise** (ma lāz´) *n.* vague bodily or emotional discomfort or uneasiness
    Tina could tell by her own *malaise* that she had contracted her daughter's cold.
    syn: illness; distress; discontent   *ant: comfort; relief; peace*

12. **disingenuous** (dis in jen´ ōō əs) *adj.* insincere; calculating
    The *disingenuous* used car salesman pointed out the car's new paint job, but not that the car had been a taxicab.
    syn: duplicitous; cunning; shifty   *ant: honest; sincere; candid*

13. **crescendo** (krə shen´ dō) *n.* a gradual increase in intensity, force, or volume
    The two-month-long city police strike began a rapid rise in crime which reached a *crescendo* after two weeks.
    syn: increase; buildup   *ant: decrease; waning*

14. **intransigent** (in tran´ sə jənt) *adj.* uncompromising; refusing to moderate
    The *intransigent* man would rather go to prison than pay income taxes.
    syn: determined; immovable; obdurate   *ant: flexible; yielding*

15. **dogged** (dô´ gid) *adj.* unrelenting; persistent
    Obsessed with his experiment, the *dogged* scientist locked himself in his laboratory and worked for three days with little rest.
    syn: driven; steadfast; unwavering   *ant: hesitating; vacillating*

Exercise I

Words in Context

From the list below, supply the words needed to complete the paragraph. Some words will not be used.

canard	**requisite**	**bulwark**	**dogged**
simian	**crescendo**	**intransigent**	

1. The Colonel had explained that it was _____ for the platoon to hold the line that night, and, despite taking heavy casualties, the _____ soldiers repelled the overwhelming enemy forces as ordered. Eventually, the enemy's attack reached its _____; McIntyre and Carson had to abandon their foxhole and retreat to the _____, where the rest of the platoon had taken cover. The retreat was not an easy task: bullets and shrapnel whizzed by the _____ soldiers as they leapt over bushes, dodged trees, and crawled through open areas in an attempt to evade enemy fire.

From the list below, supply the words needed to complete the paragraph. Some words will not be used.

wont	**cortege**	**crescendo**	**impresario**
disingenuous	**canard**	**demotic**	

2. Bernadette, the most sought-after singer in the music industry, hired a[n] _____ assistant who was talented at fabricating believable _____ in order to mislead the nosy reporters and paparazzi. Bernadette, unlike many stars, did not travel with a _____ comprising makeup artists, groupies, and bodyguards, so it was easier for her to avoid tabloid reporters and mobs of fans. Despite having amassed a fortune after her latest album went platinum, Bernadette did not buy a mansion or a fleet of cars; she simply tried to live the _____ life to which she was accustomed. She routinely rejected the offers of the most prominent _____ in the entertainment industry, who in turn threatened to take her fame away as fast as she gained it. Bernadette usually responded with a simple, "Go ahead."

From the list below, supply the words needed to complete the paragraph. Some words will not be used.

wont	bulwark	etymology	solecism
demotic	simian	malaise	

3.   Bobby was pale this morning and obviously suffering from some sort of _____, but by the afternoon, he was back to performing his _____ antics and driving his mother to the brink of insanity. The weather was _____ to improve soon, so Bobby could then take his energy to the back yard, where there were fewer things to break.

"Mommy, I was sick this morning, but I'm feeling gooder now." Jane corrected her son's _____:

"You're feeling *better* now."

"That's what I just said," said Bobby as the long leaves of a houseplant caught his attention. Jane shook her head. She didn't care if Bobby knew the _____ of every word he spoke, but she definitely wanted him to speak well.

Exercise II

Sentence Completion

Complete the sentence in a way that shows you understand the meaning of the italicized vocabulary word.

1.   The *dogged* rescue workers spent hours trying to...

2.   The father remained *intransigent* when his daughter asked...

3.   The band's *crescendo* at the end of their hit song...

4.   The clever villain had a *disingenuous* plan to...

5.   To determine the cause of her *malaise*, Jennifer decided to...

6.   The children sculpted a huge *bulwark* out of snow that would...

7.   *Requisite* items for the camping trip include...

8.   When the popular band canceled its show, the *impresario* had to...

9.   The strange rodent had *simian* characteristics that helped it to...

10. The politician claimed that her *demotic* background would help her election because...

11. During their first encounter with the mysterious tribal leader, the vastly outnumbered explorers hoped that a *solecism* in behavior would not cause...

12. The prince's *cortege* consisted of...

13. To learn about the *etymology* of a word, you might...

14. Your houseplant is *wont* to die if you...

15. Debbie, who is a career con artist, used a *canard* to...

Exercise III

Roots, Prefixes, and Suffixes

Study the entries and answer the questions that follow.

The root *plic* means "fold."
The root *lig* means "connect" or "bind."
The root *solv* means "loosen."
The prefix *ex* means "out."
The prefix *re* means "back" or "again."
The prefix *ab* means "away from."
The prefix *ob* means "toward" or "against."

1. *Using literal translations as guidance, define the following words without using a dictionary.*

   A. absolve   D. resolve
   B. explicate E. applicate
   C. oblige   F. ligament

2. The root *plex* and the suffix *ply* share the same origin as the root *plic*. List as many words as you can think of that contain the root *plex* or the suffix *ply*.

3. *Solu* is another form of *solv*. List as many words as you can think of that contain the root *solu*.

4. *Com* means "together," and it changes to *col* when placed before a word that begins with an *l*. The English word that literally means "bind to-gether" is _____ (the suffix *ate* is a Latin ending for verbs).

5. List as many words as you can think of that contain the root *solv*.

Exercise IV

Inference

Complete the sentences by inferring information about the italicized word from its context.

1. If the faltering business doesn't experience a *crescendo* in sales, the company will probably...

2. Someone who omits even one *requisite* step in assembling a bicycle should not be surprised if...

3. If the amount of your paycheck is less than usual, then you will probably be *wont* to...

Exercise V

Writing

Here is a writing prompt similar to the one you will find on the writing portion of the ACT.

The long term health of a generation is at risk in America, not because of floods or locusts or global warming, but because of simple overindulgence. America is at the height of a obesity epidemic.

Previous generations who, in youth, lacked the many technological distractions that the present generation enjoys, tend to blame sedentary lifestyles and self-indulgence for obesity. Children once explored nature freely and walked or bicycled daily from one end of town to the next. Children now spend a mind-numbing seven hours a day surfing the Internet, watching television, and playing video games. Roaming forests and fields simply isn't a realistic alternative when tracts of wilderness post *NO TRESPASSING* signs, or when the land around the old fishing hole has become host to a housing development. New roads and neighborhoods often lack sidewalks for easy foot or bicycle travel.

The contradictory part of the epidemic is that we know more now about human physiology and the benefits of diet and exercise than at any other time in human history. Forcing people to diet and exercise would be tyranny, but there is little doubt that people now, more than ever, need motivation to spend less time on the couch and more on their feet.

What incentives would entice the youth of America to turn off the television, abandon social networking sites, and get back outside to do real, healthy things? Has something changed during the last few decades, other than necessity, that has caused so many people to become digital hermits?

Pinpoint your feelings on the general health of your generation and whether it is a legitimate problem. Write a speech to be delivered at a youth exposition that describes why American's lack of fitness is a problem and whether or not it is related to the plugged-in status of so many people. Most importantly, include a minimum of one detailed solution, or a well-developed argument as to why no solution is necessary.

Thesis: Write a one-sentence response to the above statement. Make certain this sentence offers a clear statement of your position.

Example: The waning physical health of a generation leads to decreased mental heath, and the only solution will be to mandate activity through school programs.

_____

_____

Organizational Plan: If your thesis is the point on which you want to end, where does your essay need to begin? List the points of development that are inevitable in leading your reader from your beginning point to your end point. This is your outline.

1. _____

2. _____

3. _____

Draft: Use your thesis as both your beginning and your end. Following your outline, write a good first draft of your essay. Remember to support all of your points with examples, facts, references to reading, etc.

Review and revise: Exchange essays with a classmate. Using the scoring guide for Organization on page 240, score your partner's essay (while he or she scores yours). Focus on the organizational plan and the use of language conventions. If necessary, rewrite your essay to improve the organizational plan and your use of language.

Exercise VI

English Practice

Improving Paragraphs
Read the following passage and then choose the best revision for the underlined portions of the paragraph. The questions will require you to make decisions regarding the revision of the reading selection. Some revisions are not of actual mistakes, but will improve the clarity of the writing.

[1]

(1) If someone asked you which professional sport has the most interesting athletes, what would you say? (2) Terrell Owens, Deion Sanders and even Terry Bradshaw hail from the National Football League. (3) Larry Bird, Michael Jordan, and Shaquille O'Neill all play hoops. (4) The <u>fiery temper of</u>[1] Eddie Belfour, Jeremy Roenick, and Marty McSorley exist only on ice rinks. (5) But what about <u>"baseball?"</u>[2] (6) Baseball is a sport usually played in the summer. (7) Most professional baseball players seem <u>to effect</u>[3] relaxed demeanors, and the nature of the sport disallows the extremes that one might observe at a football game or a rugby match; however, one of the most unusual personalities ever to play sports did play baseball, and his name was Jimmy Piersall.

1. A. NO CHANGE
   B. fired temper of
   C. fiery temper for
   D. fiery tempers of

2. F. NO CHANGE
   G. "baseball"?
   H. baseball?
   J. baseball.

3. A. NO CHANGE
   B. to affect
   C. to infect
   D. to affectively

4. Which sentence should be removed from paragraph 1?
   F. sentence 1
   G. sentence 2
   H. sentence 4
   J. sentence 6

[2]

(8) Unfortunately, Jimmy's rookie season was cut short by a nervous breakdown, which gave him a reputation for mental <u>instability, that followed</u>[5] him throughout his career. (9) Piersall began his major league baseball career in 1952 with the Boston Red Sox. (10) In 1950 and 1951, Piersall compiled batting averages of .346 and .339 respectively for Boston's minor league team

in Birmingham, <u>Alabama however, Piersall</u>[6] was a centerfielder for Birmingham, and the Red Sox already had a major league star in center field—Dom DiMaggio, brother of the legendary Joe DiMaggio. (11) Piersall switched to shortstop so that he could join the major league club, but Piersall's accomplishments on the field were overshadowed by his erratic, albeit laughable, behavior.

5. A. NO CHANGE
   B. instability that followed
   C. instability which followed
   D. instability which follows

6. F. NO CHANGE
   G. Alabama however, Piersall
   H. Alabama; but Piersall
   J. Alabama however; Piersall

7. Which change best improves the chronology of paragraph 2?
   A. Exchange sentences 10 and 11.
   B. Move sentence 8 to the end of the paragraph.
   C. Rewrite sentence 10 in the active voice.
   D. Exchange sentences 8 and 10.

[3]

(12) <u>Irregardless of</u>[8] Piersall's relative success at bat, his crazy behavior made headlines more often than his statistics did. (13) During his rookie year, Piersall made waves by brawling with New York <u>Yankee, Billy Martin,</u>[9] in the clubhouse tunnel. (14) From 1953 onward, Jimmy stood out as a ballplayer by racking up hits and home runs, but his reputation of eccentricity continued to follow him. (15) On July 23, 1960, the day after a game in which Jimmy hit two home runs, he was ejected from a game for an unusual reason. (16) During two of Ted Williams's at-bats for Boston, Piersall, then playing for Cleveland performed a "war dance" in center field meant to distract Williams. (17) The umpires tolerated Jimmy's clowning until the eighth inning before they ejected him. (18) This, however, was not the most infamous incident in Piersall's career.

8. F. NO CHANGE
   G. Regarding
   H. Irregardless,
   J. Regardless of

9. A. NO CHANGE
   B. Yankee: Billy Martin,
   C. Yankee Billy Martin
   D. Yankee, Billy Martin

10. Paragraph 3 is missing a comma. It should be placed
    F. after *waves* in sentence 13
    G. after *1953* in sentence 14
    H. after *game* in sentence 15
    J. after *Cleveland* in sentence 16

[4]

(19) Jimmy Piersall <u>hit one home run while playing in the National League only</u>.[11] (20) But most of his career was spent with the Red Sox, the Indians, and the California Angels, his most famous home run was the one he hit with the New York Mets—also the 100th of his career. (21) After Jimmy watched the ball leave the stadium, he <u>runs around</u>[12] the bases backwards, which successfully irritated both Jimmy's manager and the baseball commissioner, not to mention the opposing pitcher. (22) A few days later, the Mets released Piersall, and he signed with his last team, the Angels.

11. A. NO CHANGE
   B. only hit one home run while playing in the National League
   C. hit only one home run while playing in the National League
   D. hit one home run while only playing in the National League

12. F. NO CHANGE
   G. had run around
   H. runs around
   J. ran around

13. Which correction best corrects a word usage error in sentence 20?
   A. Replace *Angels* with *Angles*.
   B. Replace *But* with *Although*.
   C. Use the name *Jimmy* instead of a pronoun.
   D. Replace the dash with a semicolon.

[5]

(23) Athletes like Babe Ruth, Magic Johnson, Wayne Gretzky, and Emmitt Smith will be remembered for their accomplishments on the courts, fields, and rinks where their sports are played. (24) Records for home runs, batting averages, points per game, rushing yards, in the memories of true sports fans. (25) Other athletes will be remembered in other <u>ways the ways</u>[14] in which their unorthodox mannerisms amuse and bewilder fans. (26) Jimmy Piersall was an eccentric and memorable personality both on and off the field, and his name will long be a diverting chapter in the annals of baseball.

14. F. NO CHANGE
   G. ways—the ways
   H. ways. The ways
   J. ways, the ways,

15. Sentence 24 is an example of a
   A. comma splice.
   B. run-on sentence.
   C. fragment.
   D. pronoun-noun agreement error.

Vocabulary
Power Plus
for the **ACT**
Vocabulary,
Reading, and Writing
Exercises for High Scores

Lesson Twelve

1. **propensity** (prə pen´ si tē) *n.* a tendency
   Sheila nurtured her *propensity* for hiking by relocating to the mountains.
   syn: inclination; predisposition; penchant   *ant: aversion*

2. **condescending** (kon di send´ ing) *adj.* displaying superiority;
   patronizing
   The young employee never grew accustomed to his bosses' *condescending*
   remarks.
   syn: denigrating; degrading   *ant: respectful; honorable*

3. **compunction** (kəm pungk´ shən) *n.* an uneasiness caused by guilt; a
   qualm
   Matt felt no *compunction* about stealing office supplies from work.
   syn: regret

4. **sepulcher** (se´ pəl kər) *n.* a tomb or burial chamber
   The deceased baron was placed in a foreboding *sepulcher* at the edge of
   the cemetery.
   syn: crypt; catacomb; mausoleum

5. **bellicose** (be´ li kōs) *adj.* warlike; inclined to fight
   Many of the crewmen were *bellicose* fellows looking for trouble.
   syn: pugnacious; belligerent; hostile   *ant: mild; passive; peaceful*

6. **pulchritude** (pəl´ krə tōōd) *n.* physical beauty
   Milton was so taken by Lauren's *pulchritude* that he couldn't respond
   when she greeted him.
   syn: loveliness; allure   *ant: ugliness; repulsiveness*

7. **wizened** (wiz´ ənd) *adj.* shriveled or withered from age or illness
   The *wizened* old captain had the craggy face of one who had spent a lifetime at sea.
   syn: shrunken; gnarled   *ant: sturdy; robust; stalwart*

8. **rhapsodize** (rap´ sə dīz) *v.* to express oneself enthusiastically
   She couldn't wait to go to work and *rhapsodize* about her recent engagement.
   syn: rave

9. **physiognomy** (fiz ē og´ nə mē) *n.* facial features
His *physiognomy* revealed that he was a person who had done a lot of laughing throughout his life.
syn: countenance; visage

10. **voluble** (vol´ yə bəl) *adj.* talkative
The *voluble* woman was obviously comfortable speaking in front of people.
syn: garrulous; fluent   *ant: quiet; introverted*

11. **revel** (rev´ əl) *v.* to enjoy; to take pleasure in
The home team *reveled* in the glory of winning the championship.
syn: bask; delight; indulge   *ant: grieve; lament*

12. **umbrage** (um´ brij) *n.* feeling of offense; resentment
Widespread *umbrage* at the new law prompted legislators to re-evaluate it.
syn: displeasure; ire; anger   *ant: delight; pleasure*

13. **epiphany** (i pif´ ə nē) *n.* a revelation; sudden knowledge or insight
During an *epiphany*, John realized what he had been doing wrong throughout most of his adult life.

14. **assiduous** (ə sij´ ōō əs) *adj.* diligent; persistent
The *assiduous* builder finally completed his home after six years of construction.
syn: persevering; industrious   *ant: lazy; negligent*

15. **panacea** (pan ə sē´ ə) *n.* a cure-all; a remedy for all diseases
Some grandmothers believe that chicken soup is a *panacea* for almost any ailment.
syn: elixir; nostrum

Exercise I

Words in Context

From the list below, supply the words needed to complete the paragraph. Some words will not be used.

bellicose	physiognomy	wizened	condescending
sepulcher	umbrage	rhapsodize	

1. My _____ grandfather Sam had lost his eyesight years ago, but that did not affect his ability to _____ about politics as long as someone was around to listen; however, as age took his health, he became _____ toward anyone who he thought treated him in a[n] _____ way. He knew, deep down, that his failing health was a part of the natural order of things, but he took _____ at the attempts of nurses or children to help him when he really didn't need help.

From the list below, supply the words needed to complete the paragraph. Some words will not be used.

physiognomy	bellicose	pulchritude	panacea
revel	propensity	assiduous	

2. Aunt Carol, who had the grace and _____ of a ballerina when she was younger, believes that cucumber paste is a[n] _____ that clears up any wrinkles or blemishes. Each morning and night, the _____ woman applies the slimy paste, lets it set for an hour, and then removes it, half expecting to see the _____ of a twenty-year-old returning her stare from the mirror. Though disappointed daily, Carol _____ in the belief that perhaps the miracle paste just needs a few more weeks before it begins to have an effect.

From the list below, supply the words needed to complete the paragraph. Some words will not be used.

epiphany	rhapsodize	compunction	sepulcher
revel	propensity	voluble	

3. Dr. Ramus had a[n] _____ for being in the right place at the right time, but he was in total disbelief when his team unearthed the ancient _____ rumored to contain the remains of one of the greatest rulers in history. Upon sight of the limestone slab, the normally _____ professor fell silent, unable to respond to the questions of his many assistants. He experienced a brief _____ as he gazed at the markings on the stone; somehow everything leading up to the discovery—the many letdowns and roadblocks—seemed to make sense. However, after discovering the equivalent of the Holy Grail for his field of study, the doctor had no _____ about desecrating the ancient tomb by opening it in the name of science.

Exercise II

Sentence Completion

Complete the sentence in a way that shows you understand the meaning of the italicized vocabulary word.

1. Though he had worked in an office for the last ten years, Bert had the *physiognomy* of...

2. Marcy, obsessed with her own *pulchritude*, spent hours...

3. Applicants for the telemarketing job cannot have any *compunction* about...

4. Some people believe that aloe is a natural *panacea* for...

5. Jodi hoped to have an *epiphany* in which she...

6. The *voluble* child was always ready to...

7. After seeing the students' test results, the teacher *rhapsodized* about...

8. Luke's *propensity* for drawing helped him to become...

9. The mountain climber stopped to *revel* in the...

10. Your *condescending* attitude makes it appear as though you...

11. When thousands of viewers took *umbrage* at the new sitcom, the network executives...

12. Many pyramids were actually *sepulchers* for...

13. With long, continuous, *assiduous* effort, anyone can...

14. The family waited for their *wizened* grandfather to...

15. Tom has been extremely *bellicose* ever since the day...

Exercise III

Roots, Prefixes, and Suffixes

Study the entries and answer the questions that follow.

The root *lex* means "word."
The root *leg* means "to read."
The root *script* means "write."
The suffix *graph* means "writing."
The prefix *dys* means "bad" or "difficult."
The prefix *in* means "in" or "not."
The suffix *ion* means "the act of."

1. *Using literal translations as guidance, define the following words without using a dictionary.*

   A. lexicography   D. dyslexic
   B. illegible   E. lexicon
   C. inscription   F. script

2. Sulla, a brutal dictator of ancient Rome, invented a method of writing the names of his enemies and publishing them before (*pro* means "before") all citizens; enemies on his list were marked for punishment or death. What is the word for this act of writing and publishing? Hint: the suffix *graph* is Greek; Romans spoke in Latin.

3. The root *pep* means "to digest." What is another word that means *indigestion* or "bad digestion"?

4. What form of carbon gets its name from its use as a material used for writing?

5. List as many words as you can think of that contain the root *script*.

6. List as many words as you can think of that contain the prefix *dys*.

Exercise IV

Inference

Complete the sentences by inferring information about the italicized word from its context.

1. A mediocre player might take *umbrage* at the coach's decision to...

2. Someone with a *propensity* for making people laugh might consider...

3. If you are an *assiduous* student, you usually...

Exercise V

Critical Reading

Below is a reading passage followed by several multiple-choice questions similar to the ones you will encounter on the ACT. Carefully read the passage and choose the best answer for each of the questions.

The passage is an excerpt from "Walking," an essay written in 1862 by Henry David Thoreau (1817-1862). In the passage, Thoreau reflects upon one of the greatest freedoms available to humankind: walking in nature.

My vicinity affords many good walks; and though for so many years I have walked almost every day, and sometimes for several days together, I have not yet exhausted them. An absolutely new prospect is a great happiness, and I can still get this any afternoon. Two or three hours' walking will carry me to as strange a
5 country as I expect ever to see. A single farmhouse which I had not seen before is sometimes as good as the dominions of the King of Dahomey. There is in fact a sort of harmony discoverable between the capabilities of the landscape within a circle of ten miles' radius, or the limits of an afternoon walk, and the threescore years and ten of human life. It will never become quite familiar to you.
10 Nowadays almost all man's improvements, so called, as the building of houses, and the cutting down of the forest and of all large trees, simply deform the landscape, and make it more and more tame and cheap. A people who would begin by burning the fences and let the forest stand! I saw the fences half consumed, their ends lost in the middle of the prairie, and some worldly miser with a surveyor
15 looking after his bounds, while heaven had taken place around him, and he did not see the angels going to and fro, but was looking for an old post-hole in the midst of paradise. I looked again, and saw him standing in the middle of a boggy stygian fen, surrounded by devils, and he had found his bounds without a doubt, three little stones, where a stake had been driven, and looking nearer, I saw that the Prince of
20 Darkness was his surveyor.

I can easily walk ten, fifteen, twenty, any number of miles, commencing at my own door, without going by any house, without crossing a road except where the fox and the mink do: first along by the river, and then the brook, and then the meadow and the wood-side. There are square miles in my vicinity which have no
25 inhabitant. From many a hill I can see civilization and the abodes of man afar. The farmers and their works are scarcely more obvious than woodchucks and their burrows. Man and his affairs, church and state and school, trade and commerce, and manufactures and agriculture, even politics, the most alarming of them all—I am pleased to see how little space they occupy in the landscape. Politics is but a
30 narrow field, and that still narrower highway yonder leads to it. I sometimes direct the traveler thither. If you would go to the political world, follow the great road— follow that market—man, keep his dust in your eyes, and it will lead you straight to it; for it, too, has its place merely, and does not occupy all space. I pass from it as from a bean-field into the forest, and it is forgotten. In one half-hour I can walk off
35 to some portion of the earth's surface where a man does not stand from one year's end to another, and there, consequently, politics are not, for they are but as the cigar-smoke of a man.

The village is the place to which the roads tend, a sort of expansion of the highway, as a lake of a river. It is the body of which roads are the arms and legs—a
40 trivial or quadrivial place, the thoroughfare and ordinary of travelers. The word is from the Latin villa, which together with via, "a way," or more anciently ved and vella, Varro derives from veho, "to carry," because the villa is the place to and from which things are carried. They who got their living by teaming were said vellaturam facere. Hence, too, apparently, the Latin word vilis and our vile; also villain. This
45 suggests what kind of degeneracy villagers are liable to. They are wayworn by the travel that goes by and over them, without traveling themselves.

Some do not walk at all; others walk in the highways; a few walk across lots. Roads are made for horses and men of business. I do not travel in them much, comparatively, because I am not in a hurry to get to any tavern or grocery or livery-
50 stable or depot to which they lead. I am a good horse to travel, but not from choice a roadster. The landscape-painter uses the figures of men to mark a road. He would not make that use of my figure. I walk out into a Nature such as the old prophets and poets, Menu, Moses, Homer, Chaucer, walked in. You may name it America, but it is not America: neither Americus Vespucius, nor Columbus, nor the rest were
55 the discoverers of it. There is a truer account of it in mythology than in any hi-story of America, so called, that I have seen.
[. . .]
At present, in this vicinity, the best part of the land is not private property; the landscape is not owned, and the walker enjoys comparative freedom. But possibly the day will come when it will be partitioned off into so-called pleasure-grounds,
60 in which a few will take a narrow and exclusive pleasure only—when fences shall be multiplied, and man-traps and other engines invented to confine men to the public road, and walking over the surface of God's earth shall be construed to mean trespassing on some gentleman's grounds. To enjoy a thing exclusively is com-monly to exclude yourself from the true enjoyment of it. Let us improve our
65 opportunities, then, before the evil days come.

What is it that makes it so hard sometimes to determine whither we will walk? I believe that there is a subtle magnetism in Nature, which if we unconsciously yield

70 to it, will direct us aright. It is not indifferent to us which way we walk. There is a
right way; but we are very liable from heedlessness and stupidity to take the wrong
one. We would fain take that walk, never yet taken by us through this actual world,
which is perfectly symbolical of the path which we love to travel in the interior and
ideal world; and sometimes, no doubt, we find it difficult to choose our direction,
because it does not yet exist distinctly in our idea.

1. The metaphor in paragraph 2 suggests that
    A. the devil probably set fire to the fence to harass the landowner.
    B. the man who owns the fence is selling his soul to the devil.
    C. the surveyor is angry about losing his fence to a fire.
    D. the landowner is standing in paradise, but is blind to it.

2. According to paragraph 4, the author thinks very little of
    F. the beauty of nature.
    G. undeveloped countryside.
    H. the benefits of village life.
    J. walking through woods instead of roads.

3. The following quote best relates to which example situation?

    "To enjoy a thing exclusively is commonly to exclude yourself from
    the true enjoyment of it."

    A. Many people feel guilty when given the opportunity to enjoy themselves.
    B. Someone who builds a nice fence will soon fail to notice it.
    C. The wealthy squander their fortunes on wildlife conservation causes.
    D. Cities build wonderful parks, but prevent people from walking on
       the grass.

4. As used in line 17, *stygian* most nearly means
    F. swampy and dank.
    G. hot and humid.
    H. covered with vegetation.
    J. relating to the underworld.

5. The author's attitude toward the achievements of mankind can be
    described as one of
    A. dismissiveness.
    B. rudeness.
    C. contempt.
    D. praise.

6. Choose the statement that best summarizes the author's description of politics.
    F. balanced and typically fair
    G. irritating and fleeting
    H. imbalanced but harmless
    J. intrusive and obscure

7. The relationship between the words *vile* and *village* is appropriate, according to the author, because
    A. trading is an unhealthy living.
    B. villages attract wayward criminals.
    C. lakes are too big to govern.
    D. a lack of travel has corrupted villagers.

8. Which place best describes the ideal walking destination for the author?
    F. virgin wilderness, beyond all settlement
    G. a path running alongside a river
    H. wherever the road leads him
    J. a horse farm within walking distance of the village

9. Choose the statement that best paraphrases lines 52-56.
    A. Only native Americans have claim to America.
    B. America has a rich and unknown ancient history.
    C. The names and histories people assign to nature are meaningless.
    D. Exploration is required to give identity to the land.

10. The author of the passage would agree that
    F. it is important to designate a travel destination.
    G. people should maintain journals wherever they go.
    H. cities and monuments are the best destinations for travelers.
    J. some form of travel in one's life is important.

Vocabulary Power Plus for the ACT
Vocabulary, Reading, and Writing Exercises for High Scores

Lesson Thirteen

1. **implicate** (im´ pli kāt) *v.* to involve or connect unfavorably
   Jeff *implicated* his friend in the crime by hiding in the friend's basement.
   syn: entangle; incriminate   *ant: extricate; dissociate*

2. **analgesic** (an əl jē´ zik) *n.* a medication to reduce or eliminate pain
   I took an *analgesic* to relieve my headache.
   syn: painkiller   *ant: irritant*

3. **turpitude** (tûr´ pi tōōd) *n.* wickedness; vileness
   In the lawless frontier town, newcomers were often shocked by the
   turpitude of the residents and patrons.
   syn: depravity; wantonness; decadence   *ant: purity; goodness*

4. **discretionary** (di skresh´ ə ner ē) *adj.* left to one's own judgment
   Part of the grant included funds to be used specifically for research, but
   the remainder of the funds were for *discretionary* use.
   syn: elective; nonobligatory; unrestricted   *ant: mandatory; obligatory*

5. **flummox** (flum´ əks) *v.* to confuse; to perplex
   The student's profound question *flummoxed* both the professor and the
   class.
   syn: bewilder; baffle; perplex   *ant: clarify; simplify*

6. **unpalatable** (un pal´ ə tə bəl) *adj.* unpleasant to the taste or the mind
   The movie director deleted a scene that he thought would be *unpalatable*
   to certain audiences.
   syn: displeasing; objectionable; offensive   *ant: pleasing; agreeable*

7. **histrionics** (his trē on´ iks) *n.* exaggerated emotional behavior
   Jane was prepared for her parents' *histrionics* when she announced her
   engagement to a man they detested.
   syn: theatrics; dramatics; hysterics

8. **draconian** (drā kō´ nē ən) *adj.* extremely harsh; very severe
   The *draconian* rules and punishments at the prison are intended to
   prevent violence.
   syn: callous; merciless   *ant: lenient*

9. **noisome** (noi´ səm) *adj.* disgusting; offensive to the senses
Despite its *noisome* odor, the imported cheese is supposedly very tasty.
syn: nauseating; fetid   *ant: delightful; pleasing*

10. **punctilious** (pənk til´ ē əs) *adj.* attentive to details in conduct or action
The *punctilious* reader frequently contacted publishers to point out
typographical errors in books.
syn: conscientious; particular; meticulous   *ant: careless; inattentive*

11. **veritable** (ver´ i tə bəl) *adj.* authentic; genuine
The apple tree was a *veritable* feast for the hungry deer.
syn: indubitable; bona fide   *ant: bogus; counterfeit*

12. **florid** (flôr´ id) *adj.* rosy or red in color
His face turned a *florid* shade when he became angry.
syn: ruddy; reddish; flushed

13. **fractious** (frak´ shəs) *adj.* unruly; disruptive
The *fractious* man always had something to complain about during town
meetings.
syn: stubborn; difficult   *ant: temperate*

14. **moribund** (môr´ ə bund) *adj.* near death; about to die
The *moribund* patient asked his niece to come closer to hear his last
request.
syn: dying; perishing   *ant: thriving; flourishing*

15. **conflagration** (kon flə grā´ shən) *n.* a large, destructive fire
The *conflagration* that began with a scented candle reduced the entire
city block to ashes.
syn: blaze; inferno

Exercise I

Words in Context

From the list below, supply the words needed to complete the paragraph. Some words will not be used.

veritable	implicate	histrionics	unpalatable
florid	punctilious	turpitude	

1. Two consecutive nights of Shakespearean theater was a[n] _____ prize for Winona, who prefers the realism of classical actors to the _____ of most television actors. _____ members of the audience, such as Winona, noticed that good actors can even make their faces turn _____ with rage or great sadness. Winona often wonders if actors rely upon _____, personal memories to fuel the emotions they portray on the stage.

From the list below, supply the words needed to complete the paragraph. Some words will not be used.

veritable	discretionary	moribund	draconian
analgesic	flummox	noisome	

2. Randy's decision to go camping was entirely _____, but after the experience, he knew that he wouldn't be returning to the great outdoors again in the near future. On the first day, a bee stung him near his eye and caused it to swell shut. That night, as he applied a topical _____ to reduce the pain of the sting, he was overwhelmed by the _____ odor of a skunk—a skunk in his tent.

    Once he'd taken an emergency bath in the river, after being sprayed by the skunk, Randy helped his family pack up the car and leave, three days early. Randy's bad luck on the trip _____ him; he had never had such a miserable time in the wilderness. He thought that the trip might renew his _____ sense of adventure after working eight years in an office cubicle as a computer network administrator, but instead it caused him to think of how great it would be to go home to a clean shower, relax on the sofa, and maybe watch a movie in his skunk and insect-free living room.

From the list below, supply the words needed to complete the paragraph. Some words will not be used.

implicate	florid	conflagration	fractious
turpitude	draconian	discretionary	

3.   Police suspected arson as the cause of the _____ that destroyed the apartment building, and they were thankful that the criminal's _____ had not killed anyone. A massive investigation quickly produced several suspects in the case, one of whom was _____ in the crime by mysterious burns on his hands, as though he had been too close to open flames. When the name of the suspect leaked to the general public, police had to restrain a[n] _____ mob from destroying his house in an attempt to bestow some sort of _____ justice on the man.

Exercise II

Sentence Completion

Complete the sentence in a way that shows you understand the meaning of the italicized vocabulary word.

1. The previously calm peace talks turned into a *veritable* shouting match when...

2. You can inadvertently start a *conflagration* if you...

3. The boss assumed full responsibility for the mistake even though he could have *implicated*...

4. Jokingly, the identical twins sometimes *flummoxed* their parents by...

5. Few people were capable of surviving the *draconian* conditions of...

6. Jason winced at the *noisome* sight of...

7. The wine had a deep, *florid* color resembling that of...

8. The teacher asked the angry drama student to save her *histrionics* for...

9. The *fractious* patrons of the tavern near the wharf were known to...

10. The school will provide sports equipment, but players have the *discretionary* option to...

11. The doctor prescribed an *analgesic* to...

12. The *punctilious* artist was famous for his tiny...

13. Some say that publishing books on paper is a *moribund* practice because digital texts will...

14. "This is *unpalatable*," gasped the chef after...

15. The *turpitude* of a few elected officials has the potential to...

Exercise III

Roots, Prefixes, and Suffixes

Study the entries and answer the questions that follow.

The root *hib* means "have" or "hold."
The roots *cept* and *capt* mean "to take" or "to seize."
The prefix *in* means "in."
The prefix *ex* means "out."
The prefix *de* means "away from."
The prefix *pre* means "before."
The prefix *re* means "back" or "again."
The prefix *con* means "together."

1. Using literal translations as guidance, define the following words without using a dictionary.

   A. except   D. deception
   B. inhibit   E. exhibition
   C. precept   F. reception

2. What word comes from the *hib* root and means "to forbid"?

3. If you _____ someone's mail, then you seize it before that person receives it; however, it is illegal to take someone's mail, so the police might attempt to _____ you and put you in jail.

4. After you pay a bill, you might *take back* a document that proves that you paid. This document is called a[n] _____.

5. List as many words as you can think of that contain the prefix *pre*.

Exercise IV

Inference

Complete the sentences by inferring information about the italicized word from its context.

1. The Joneses knew that their son needed discipline, but they were afraid that the *draconian* rules at the military academy would...

2. If the concert crowd becomes *fractious*, the police might...

3. Some people believe that wearing helmets on motorcycles should be *discretionary* for riders, but others believe that...

Exercise V

Writing

Here is a writing prompt similar to the one you will find on the writing portion of the ACT.

> Even in fiction, characters who travel in time, especially to the past, generally know that famous historical events—even terrible ones—should never be altered. They understand that wars, assassinations, famines, plagues and other great tragedies rife with human suffering must be allowed to occur, ostensibly because the alternative—the new history—can always possibly be worse than the original. Many ideas, however, are postulated much more easily in fiction than when they become reality. It is easy to impose rules upon nonexistent technology; however, imagine what the interest would be in a device that suddenly had the potential to instantly change up to millions of lives for the better.
>
> Imagine for a moment that time travel is a reality, and that humankind has the option to send a single team of time travelers to the past. Should an exception to the rule be made and the team allowed to attempt to alter the outcome of some historical event? Is there anything in history so egregious that it should be allowed to be stopped in spite of the risk of changing the future?
>
> Think of historical events or decisions that have caused great conflict, pain, or suffering and decide if one should be changed. In a letter to the time travel selection board, identify the event you have selected and explain why it is worthy of interference. Argue why it would be worth the risk to change a single event. If you disagree with intervention, argue against changing history and explain the consequences of tampering with events. If you choose to argue against time travel, be sure to support your argument with example scenarios.

Thesis: Write a one-sentence response to the above assignment. Make certain this sentence offers a clear statement of your position.

> *Example: Though the final choice should be left to a worldwide vote, the event that has caused the greatest number of deaths in recent years should be the target of intervention.*

_____

_____

Organizational Plan: If your thesis is the point on which you want to end, where does your essay need to begin? List the points of development that are inevitable in leading your reader from your beginning point to your end point. This list is your outline.

1. _____

2. _____

3. _____

Draft: Use your thesis as both your beginning and your end. Following your outline, write a good first draft of your essay. Remember to support all of your points with examples, facts, references to reading, etc.

Review and revise: Exchange essays with a classmate. Using the scoring guide for Development on page 241, score your partner's essay (while he or she scores yours). Focus on the development of ideas and the use of language conventions. If necessary, rewrite your essay to improve the development of ideas and your use of language.

Exercise VI

English Practice

Identifying Sentence Errors
Identify the errors in the following sentences. Choose the answer that fixes the error. If the sentence contains no error, select NO CHANGE.

1. Many students look much different than they did last <u>semester; it's</u> probably because of their new outfits.
   A. NO CHANGE
   B. semester, it's
   C. semester: it's
   D. semester; its'

2. Both my <u>brother-in-laws work</u> at the same company, and they are trying to get me an interview for a job there.
   F. NO CHANGE
   G. brother-in-laws works
   H. brothers-in-law work
   J. brothers-in-laws work

3. Would you please tell the delivery <u>person to sit</u> the packages on the kitchen table? I'll pay him after I find my purse.
   A. NO CHANGE
   B. person to lie
   C. man to sit
   D. person to set

4. All members of the volunteer fire company, and even their dog, received a commendation from the mayor for <u>its enormous</u> efforts during the fund-raising drive.
   F. NO CHANGE
   G. their enormous
   H. they're enormous
   J. it's enormous

5. If I had brought enough money, I definitely <u>would of purchased</u> the car I wanted at last week's auction in Marvell, New York.
   A. NO CHANGE
   B. would of brought
   C. would have purchased
   D. could of purchased

Improving Sentences

The underlined portion of each sentence below contains some flaw. Select the answer that best corrects the flaw.

6. If you will pay close attention to what I actually say, <u>you will be able to understand my instructions more perfectly.</u>
    F. you might be able to understand my instructions more perfectly.
    G. you will understand my instructions perfectly and ably.
    H. you will be able to understand my instructions perfectly.
    J. my instructions will be able to be understood by you perfectly.

7. <u>My father objects to me playing football because of the dangers</u> inherent in any contact sport.
    A. My father objects to my playing football because of the dangers
    B. My father objects to playing football because of the dangers
    C. Because of the dangers, my father objects to me playing football
    D. My father objects to football because of the dangers

8. Most of the mowing of our lawn was done <u>by the two oldest of the three sons, my brother and I.</u>
    F. by two of the three sons, my brother and I.
    G. by the two eldest of the three sons, my brother and me.
    H. by the two elders of the three sons, my brother and me.
    J. by the oldest of the three sons, my brother and I.

9. <u>The United States, as the worlds preeminent democracy, must always protect the right's of their citizens.</u>
    A. The United States, as the world's preeminent Democracy, must always protect the right's of their citizens.
    B. The United States is the worlds' preeminent democracy, and must always protect the rights of their citizens.
    C. The United States, as the worlds preeminent democracy, must always protect it's citizen's right's.
    D. The United States, as the world's preeminent democracy, must always protect the rights of its citizens.

10. The physician says that <u>there is always the possibility that the cancer might return, but so far, there has been no signs of a recurrence.</u>

    F. there was always the possibility that the cancer might return, but so far, there has been no signs of a recurrence.

    G. there is always the possibility that the cancer might return, but so far, there was no signs of a recurrence.

    H. there is always the possibility that the cancer might return, but so far, there have been no signs of a recurrence.

    J. there always is the possibility that the cancer might return, but so far there has been not any sign of it recurring.

Vocabulary
Power Plus
for the **ACT**
Vocabulary,
Reading, and Writing
Exercises for High Scores

Lesson Fourteen

1. **protégé** (prō′ tə zhā) *n.* a person under the guidance or training of another
    When the famous artist died, his young *protégé* began a long and successful career.
    syn: apprentice   *ant: mentor*

2. **indiscernible** (in di sûr′ nə bəl) *adj.* difficult or impossible to discern or perceive
    The flaw in the paint was *indiscernible* unless you knew where to look.
    syn: imperceptible; indistinguishable; subtle   *ant: evident; noticeable; obvious*

3. **virulent** (vir′ yə lənt) *adj.* extremely infectious or poisonous
    The hospital used an incinerator to destroy any *virulent* waste.
    syn: venomous; toxic   *ant: harmless*

4. **phlegmatic** (fleg mat′ ik) *adj.* calm and unemotional
    The *phlegmatic* man didn't even smile when he saw that he had a winning lottery ticket.
    syn: apathetic; cold; unfeeling   *ant: lively; excited*

5. **artisan** (är′ ti zən) *n.* a skilled manual worker; a craftsperson
    Mike hired *artisans* from the welder's union to make repairs to the steel holding tanks.

6. **reciprocate** (ri sip′ rə kāt) *v.* to give in response to receiving something
    The teacher explained that he would *reciprocate* good classroom behavior by grading on a curve.
    syn: match

7. **tenable** (ten′ ə bəl) *adj.* rationally defensible
    After hearing the defendant's *tenable* reason for stealing the car, the jury found him not guilty.
    syn: sound; viable; credible   *ant: questionable; unbelievable*

8. **boondoggle** (bōōn′ dôg əl) *n.* an unnecessary, wasteful project
    Some people believe that building a space station is a *boondoggle* because any resulting advancements will not offset the cost of construction.

9. **curmudgeon** (kər muj´ ən) *n.* a stubborn, ill-tempered person
The old *curmudgeon* sat on the bench at the mall and complained to any one who would listen.
syn: grouch; bellyacher; killjoy

10. **moiety** (moi´ ə tē) *n.* a portion or part of something
Each of the heirs received a *moiety* of his uncle's large estate.
syn: division; piece

11. **inculcate** (in kəl´ kāt) *v.* to impress upon or teach someone by repetition
The chemistry teacher *inculcated* atomic mass values into her students until they could recite the numbers without looking at a chart.

12. **fiduciary** (fə dōō´ shē er ē) *adj.* relating to the governing of property or estate on behalf of others
Mr. Montaire has the *fiduciary* duty of controlling the family fortune until his nephew turns eighteen.

13. **repugnant** (ri pug´ nənt) *adj.* offensive; repulsive
The *repugnant* comedian depended on shock, not talent, to make a living.
syn: abhorrent; obnoxious   *ant: appealing; enjoyable; nice*

14. **opprobrium** (ə prō´ brē əm) *n.* disgrace; extreme dishonor
The vandals who desecrated the church were regarded with *opprobrium* in the years following the crime.
syn: obloquy; ignominy; shame   *ant: esteem; honor; respect*

15. **potentate** (pōt´ n tāt) *n.* a monarch; one who has great power
Diamond Jim, a real estate *potentate*, is said to own half of the state.
syn: sovereign; magnate; king   *ant: peasant; plebian; serf*

Exercise I

Words in Context

From the list below, supply the words needed to complete the paragraph. Some words will not be used.

virulent	artisan	protégé	reciprocate
inculcate	fiduciary	indiscernible	

1. To some, Kurt was a simple stonemason who built fireplaces or walls next to driveways, but James, Kurt's young _____, recognized that the aging man was a[n] _____ who worked with natural stones as an artist would work with paint. James had been Kurt's assistant for several years, and during that time, Kurt _____ Jane's fingers with the many tricks and techniques for creating impressive masonry. In time, James was able to stack and chisel stones and make the natural flaws _____, just as Kurt had done for nearly fifty years. Before Kurt passed away, he gave James _____ responsibility of the business, pleased that the ancient craft would last for another generation.

From the list below, supply the words needed to complete the paragraph. Some words will not be used.

repugnant	protégé	reciprocate	boondoggle
phlegmatic	tenable	curmudgeon	

2. Agnes scolded her husband of fifty years for being such a[n] _____.
    "Your constant griping is _____; it's no wonder no one wants to visit any more. Unlike your grumpy friends, our grandchildren don't care to _____ your incessant complaining with complaints of their own. Yes, dear, you make some _____ arguments, but sometimes you need to be more optimistic." Harold, briefly _____ and unresponsive, exhaled in antipathy and continued to watch a rerun of his favorite television game show. He had to catch himself before yelling at the contestant he knew would lose the big prize at the end.

From the list below, supply the words needed to complete the paragraph. Some words will not be used.

curmudgeon   virulent   boondoggle   moiety
potentate   tenable   opprobrium

3.   P.J. Tucker, the _____ at the helm of the twelfth-largest corporation on Earth, squinted when he saw the company's fiscal data for the quarter. A recent series of acquisitions had turned into a[n] _____, because two of the newly acquired companies had failed miserably. P.J. knew that if hints of the loss got out, the _____ rumor would spread through the corporation like a disease. Workers, each of whom had contributed a[n] _____ of his or her life to the success of the company, would now be forced to endure widespread cutbacks and layoffs. P.J. knew that thousands of his employees would view him with _____ for years as the wealthy executive who fired thousands of workers to protect his own fortune.

Exercise II

Sentence Completion

Complete the sentence in a way that shows you understand the meaning of the italicized vocabulary word.

1. Jerry, the spatula *potentate* of the kitchen utensil industry, had contracts with...

2. During construction of the mansion, woodworking *artisans* were hired to...

3. Kim felt that she deserved at least a *moiety* of credit for the team's championship season because...

4. The scientist's young *protégé* quickly learned...

5. When George refused to curb his *repugnant* language at work, the supervisor...

6. Half of Congress felt that the nation had a *tenable* reason for going to war, but the other half...

7. The piano teacher *inculcated* the major musical scales into her students by...

8. The Center for Disease Control quarantined the person with a *virulent* strain of Anthrax before the disease...

9. Constructing a new warehouse while sales were floundering proved to be a *boondoggle* that caused...

10. Mortimer has *fiduciary* responsibility for the charitable organization, so he decides...

11. The *curmudgeon* frequently wrote letters to the editor of the newspaper demanding...

12. During the hurricane, the *phlegmatic* ship captain showed little...

13. When his neighbor shovels snow from Joe's sidewalk, Joe *reciprocates* by...

14. The *indiscernible* stain on the carpet is noticeable only if you...

15. Though the man was found innocent in court, he lived in *opprobrium* for years because...

Exercise III

Roots, Prefixes, and Suffixes

Study the entries and answer the questions that follow.

The root *pugn* means "fight."
The root *bell* means "war."
The root *pac* means "peace."
The suffix *ious* means "full of."
The suffix *ose* means "full of."
The prefix *re* means "back" or "again."
The prefix *ante* means "before."

1. Using literal translations as guidance, define the following words without using a dictionary.

   A. repugnant   D. antebellum
   B. pacify   E. pugnacious
   C. belligerent   F. pact

2. The prefix *im* means "against," so what do you think it means to *impugn* someone's claim?

3. How do you think the Pacific Ocean got its name?

4. Someone who fights back against the rules might be called a[n]

   _____.

5. List as many words as you can think of that contain the root *pac*.

Exercise IV

Inference

Complete the sentences by inferring information about the italicized word from its context.

1. Someone who has a *virulent* cold should not...

2. Customers complained about Jake's *repugnant* behavior at the upscale restaurant when he...

3. If you fail to *reciprocate* when someone treats you well, then that person...

━━━━━

┌─────────────────────┐
Exercise V
└─────────────────────┘

Critical Reading

Below is a reading passage followed by several multiple-choice questions similar to the ones you will encounter on the ACT. Carefully read the passage and choose the best answer for each of the questions.

Joseph Conrad wrote the classic novella, "Heart of Darkness," in 1899, during the peak of the British Empire. In the story, Marlow, a steamboat captain and narrator of the tale, recounts his voyage deep into the Congo, which was a Belgian territory at the time. Marlow has the mission of contacting Kurtz, an ivory trader who works for the Belgian company deep in the Congo at the "inner station." The following excerpt from Heart of Darkness *begins with Marlow's arrival at a Belgian station thirty miles from the mouth of the Congo.*

     "There's your company's station," said the Swede, pointing to three wooden barrack-like structures on the rocky slope. "I will send your things up. Four boxes did you say? So. Farewell."

     I came upon a boiler wallowing in the grass, then found a path leading up the
5 hill. It turned aside for the boulders, and also for an undersized railway truck lying there on its back with its wheels in the air. One was off. The thing looked as dead as the carcass of some animal. I came upon more pieces of decaying machinery, a stack of rusty rails. To the left a clump of trees made a shady spot, where dark things seemed to stir feebly. I blinked, the path was steep. A horn tooted to the right, and
10 I saw the black people run. A heavy and dull detonation shook the ground, a puff of smoke came out of the cliff, and that was all. No change appeared on the face of the rock. They were building a railway. The cliff was not in the way or anything; but this objectless blasting was all the work going on.

     A slight clinking behind me made me turn my head. Six black men advanced in
15 a file, toiling up the path. They walked erect and slow, balancing small baskets full of earth on their heads, and the clink kept time with their footsteps. Black rags were wound round their loins, and the short ends behind waggled to and fro like tails. I could see every rib, the joints of their limbs were like knots in a rope; each had an iron collar on his neck, and all were connected together with a chain whose bights
20 swung between them, rhythmically clinking. Another report from the cliff made me think suddenly of that ship of war I had seen firing into a continent. It was the same kind of ominous voice; but these men could by no stretch of imagination be called enemies. They were called criminals, and the outraged law, like the bursting shells, had come to them, an insoluble mystery from the sea. All their meager breasts
25 panted together, the violently dilated nostrils quivered, the eyes stared stonily uphill. They passed me within six inches, without a glance, with that complete, death-like indifference of unhappy savages. Behind this raw matter one of the reclaimed, the product of the new forces at work, strolled despondently, carrying a rifle by its middle. He had a uniform jacket with one button off, and seeing a white

30 man on the path, hoisted his weapon to his shoulder with alacrity. This was simple
prudence, white men being so much alike at a distance that he could not tell who
I might be. He was speedily reassured, and with a large, white, rascally grin, and a
glance at his charge, seemed to take me into partnership in his exalted trust. After
all, I also was a part of the great cause of these high and just proceedings.

35   Instead of going up, I turned and descended to the left. My idea was to let that
chain gang get out of sight before I climbed the hill. You know I am not particu-larly
tender; I've had to strike and to fend off. I've had to resist and to attack sometimes—
that's only one way of resisting—without counting the exact cost, according to the
demands of such sort of life as I had blundered into. I've seen the devil of violence,

40 and the devil of greed, and the devil of hot desire; but, by all the stars! these were
strong, lusty, red-eyed devils, that swayed and drove men—men, I tell you. But as
I stood on this hillside, I foresaw that in the blinding sunshine of that land I would
become acquainted with a flabby, pretending, weak-eyed devil of a rapacious and
pitiless folly. How insidious he could be, too, I was only to find out several months

45 later and a thousand miles farther. For a moment I stood appalled, as though by a
warning. Finally I descended the hill, obliquely, towards the tree I had seen.

I avoided a vast artificial hole somebody had been digging on the slope, the
purpose of which I found it impossible to divine. It wasn't a quarry or a sandpit,
anyhow. It was just a hole. It might have been connected with the philanthropic

50 desire of giving the criminals something to do. I don't know. Then I nearly fell into
a very narrow ravine, almost no more than a scar in the hillside. I discovered that a
lot of imported drainage pipes for the settlement had been tumbled in there. There
w-asn't one that was not broken. It was a wanton smashup. At last I got under the
trees. My purpose was to stroll into the shade for a moment; but no sooner within

55 than it seemed to me I had stepped into the gloomy circle of some inferno. The
rapids were near, and an uninterrupted, uniform, headlong, rushing noise filled the
mournful stillness of the grove, where not a breath stirred, not a leaf moved, with a
mysterious sound—as though the tearing pace of the launched earth had sud-denly
become audible.

60   Black shapes crouched, lay, sat between the trees leaning against the trunks,
clinging to the earth, half coming out, half effaced within the dim light, in all the
attitudes of pain, abandonment, and despair. Another mine on the cliff went off,
followed by a slight shudder of the soil under my feet. The work was going on. The
work! And this was the place where some of the helpers had withdrawn to die.

65   They were dying slowly—it was very clear. They were not enemies, they were
not criminals, they were nothing earthly now, nothing but black shadows of disease
and starvation, lying confusedly in the greenish gloom. Brought from all the recesses
of the coast in all the legality of time contracts, lost in uncongenial surroundings,
fed on unfamiliar food, they sickened, became inefficient, and were then allowed

70 to crawl away and rest. These moribund shapes were free as air—and nearly as
thin. I began to distinguish the gleam of the eyes under the trees. Then, glancing
down, I saw a face near my hand. The black bones reclined at full length with one
shoulder against the tree, and slowly the eyelids rose and the sunken eyes looked
up at me, enormous and vacant, a kind of blind, white flicker in the depths of the

75 orbs, which died out slowly. The man seemed young—almost a boy—but you know
with them it's hard to tell. I found nothing else to do but to offer him one of my
good Swede's ship's biscuits I had in my pocket. The fingers closed slowly on it and

held—there was no other movement and no other glance. He had tied a bit of white worsted round his neck—Why? Where did he get it? Was it a badge—an
80 ornament—a charm—a propitiatory act? Was there any idea at all connected with it? It looked startling round his black neck, this bit of white thread from beyond the seas.

1. As used in line 20, *report* most nearly means
    A. account.
    B. breeze.
    C. shot.
    D. test.

2. The narrator of the passage is probably
    F. one of the enslaved workers.
    G. a white newcomer to the station.
    H. an official of the colony that he is describing.
    J. a high-ranking native worker for the station.

3. Which choice best describes the author's purpose for including the following line?

    "After all, I also was a part of the great cause of these high and just proceedings."

    A. He is demonstrating his own nationalism.
    B. He is suggesting his relief that the colony is now civilized.
    C. He is sarcastically criticizing the jurisprudence of the colonies.
    D. He is mocking the prisoners.

4. As used in line 41, *swayed* most nearly means
    F. spoke to.
    G. governed.
    H. staggered.
    J. hired.

5. To whom or what does the following quotation refer?

    "...flabby, pretending, weak-eyed devil of a rapacious and pitiless folly" (lines 43-44)

    A. to the criminals blasting rock from the cliff face
    B. to the Belgians controlling the territory
    C. to a person the narrator eventually meets
    D. to the man guarding the chain gang

6. In his use of physical description, the author of the passage suggests that eyes
   F. are often symbolic in literature.
   G. reflect man's inner nature.
   H. are unimportant to laborers.
   J. reveal one's sins.

7. As used in line 48, *divine* most nearly means
   A. neat.
   B. orderly.
   C. discover.
   D. celestial.

8. According to the passage, what characteristic does the blasting of the cliff share with the hole on the slope in paragraph 5?
   F. Both of the projects appear to be entirely unnecessary.
   G. Both of the projects were supervised by the narrator.
   H. Colonists provide the labor for both projects.
   J. Both the hole and the cliff are symbols of government.

9. In the final paragraph, the narrator declares that the people beneath the trees are not criminals because
   A. they did not have proper trials.
   B. they are political enemies, not criminals.
   C. most of them are from other nations.
   D. they do not even appear to be human.

10. According to the passage, which word best describes the narrator's feelings about the scenes he witnesses?
    F. indifference
    G. pride
    H. horror
    J. disruption

Level Twelve

REVIEW
Lessons 8–14

Exercise I

Sentence Completion

Choose the best pair of words to complete the sentence. Most choices will fit grammatically and will even make sense logically, but you must choose the pair that best fits the idea of the sentence.

1. Those who have a(n) _____ for criticizing minor grammatical errors are almost sure to be caught using _____ themselves.
   A. propensity, solecisms
   B. perquisite, toadies
   C. renunciation, sepulchers
   D. opprobrium, analgesics
   E. largesse, histrionics

2. As a(n) _____ of her position, the _____ was owed favors from some of the wealthiest and most influential celebrities in the nation.
   A. boondoggle, majordomo
   B. umbrage, bumpkin
   C. perquisite, impresario
   D. asperity, artisan
   E. recrimination, protégé

3. To save the bulk of the corporation, the _____ had no choice but to make _____ cuts to budgets and personnel, laying off thousands of employees worldwide.
   A. exegesis, voluble
   B. sepulcher, indolent
   C. epiphany, otiose
   D. potentate, draconian
   E. curmudgeon, moribund

4. The special operations soldiers were _____ in the precise steps of their secret incursion mission for weeks until the commander had absolutely no _____ about boasting about their imminent success.
   A. inculcated, compunction
   B. reciprocated, conflagration
   C. implicated, asperity
   D. corroborated, exegesis
   E. lionized, probity

5. A(n) elderly, _____ customer engaged in some completely unnecessary _____ when the restaurant refused to serve food from the breakfast menu during the lunch rush.
   A. wizened, histrionics
   B. aleatory, physiognomy
   C. bellicose, turpitude
   D. discretionary, opprobrium
   E. polemical, veneer

6. Knowing that _____ is as fleeting as youth itself, the _____ fashion model worked her way through pharmacology school to prepare for her next career.
   A. moiety, fiduciary
   B. asperity, condescending
   C. probity, orotund
   D. malaise, untenable
   E. pulchritude, assiduous

7. The _____ offered to help the hitchhiker, not realizing that the _____ drifter planned to hijack his truck.
   A. epiphany, hortatory
   B. bumpkin, disingenuous
   C. majordomo, profligate
   D. toady, unpalatable
   E. curmudgeon, florid

8. Owing to a(n) _____ alibi, the convict was incarcerated for six years before a witness _____ his story and forced the district prosecutor to conduct a new trial.
   A. phlegmatic, implicated
   B. indiscernible, vitiated
   C. untenable, corroborated
   D. voluble, depredated
   E. unimpeachable, flummoxed

Exercise II

Crossword Puzzle

Use the clues to complete the crossword puzzle. The answers consist of vocabulary words from lessons 8 through 14.

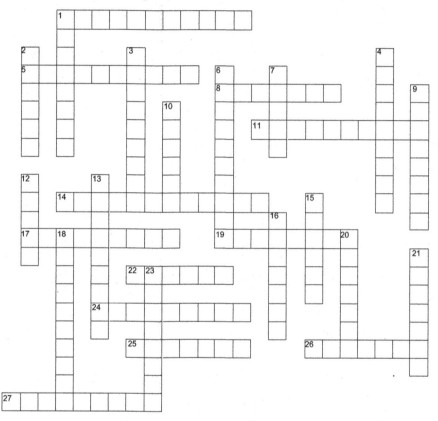

Across

1. uneasiness caused by guilt
5. disgrace; dishonor
8. to protest
11. a tip
14. insincere; calculating
17. to connect unfavorably
19. error in speech or manners
22. beneficial
24. impossible to defend
25. rationally defensible
26. childish
27. unruly; disruptive

Down

1. deserving blame
2. a portion or part
3. extremely harsh
4. wickedness
6. indirect; roundabout
7. to take pleasure in
9. wildly excited
10. useless; futile
12. indicated but not expressed
13. diligent; persistent
15. carefree
16. relating to ordinary people
18. calm and unemotional
20. vague bodily discomfort
21. a cure-all
23. an explanation of a text

Vocabulary
Power Plus
for the
ACT
Vocabulary,
Reading, and Writing
Exercises for High Scores

Lesson Fifteen

1. **prominent** (prom´ ə nənt) *adj.* very noticeable or obvious
The trunk is a *prominent* feature of an elephant.
syn: conspicuous; clear   *ant: inconspicuous*

2. **autonomy** (ô ton´ ə mē) *n.* independence
Vicky enjoys the *autonomy* of being self-employed as a freelance writer.
syn: self-rule; license; sovereignty   *ant: subordination*

3. **gustatory** (gus´ tə tôr ē) *adj.* relating to the sense of taste
The gourmet dinner lacked the *gustatory* appeal that Julie expected.

4. **chthonian** (thō´ nē ən) *adj.* pertaining to the underworld; dwelling in
or beneath the surface of the earth
The *chthonian* engraving in the tomb featured a lion guarding the gates of
the netherworld.

5. **extirpate** (ek´ stər pāt) *v.* to root out or eradicate; to destroy completely
New weeds sprouted faster than Bob could *extirpate* them.
syn: expunge; uproot; exterminate   *ant: generate; propagate*

6. **coagulate** (kō ag´ yə lāt) *v.* to change or be changed from liquid into
a thickened or solid mass
You should clean the spilled cooking grease before it *coagulates* on the
floor.
syn: congeal; solidify; curdle   *ant: liquefy*

7. **puissance** (pwē´ səns) *n.* power; might
You'll need considerable *puissance* to win the game tomorrow, so get
plenty of rest.
syn: strength; vigor   *ant: frailty; weakness*

8. **appellation** (ap ə lā´ shən) *n.* name, title, or designation
The pre-med student hoped to earn the *appellation* of "Doctor."
syn: denomination; classification

9. **peripatetic** (per ə pə te´ tik) *adj.* traveling, especially by foot
The *peripatetic* wanderer seldom passed through the same town twice.
syn: ambulant; vagabond; nomadic   *ant: stationary*

10. **misanthrope** (mis´ ən thrōp) *n.* one who hates or mistrusts humankind
The *misanthrope* never travels far from his remote cabin, and he threatens anyone who wanders near it.
ant: samaritan

11. **tutelary** (tōōt´ ə ler ē) *adj.* pertaining to guardianship
Donald had enough *tutelary* experience to be a good foster father.
syn: custodial; guardian

12. **scion** (sī´ ən) *n.* descendant; heir
The *scions* of the wealthy industrialist quickly squandered the family fortune.
syn: successor; progeny   *ant: predecessor; ancestor*

13. **jurisprudence** (jŏŏr is prōōd´ ns) *n.* the science, philosophy, and application of the law
The judge had to dismiss the case because of the prosecutor's faulty *jurisprudence.*

14. **supercilious** (sōō pər sil´ ē əs) *adj.* contemptuous; arrogant
The *supercilious* widow raised her eyebrows and looked away when I greeted her.
syn: haughty; condescending; conceited   *ant: modest; humble*

15. **malevolent** (mə lev´ ə lənt) *adj.* having ill-will; wishing harm; evil
The burglar turned and ran when he met the *malevolent* stare of a large guard dog.
syn: malicious; sinister; menacing   *ant: benevolent*

Exercise I

Words in Context

From the list below, supply the words needed to complete the paragraph. Some words will not be used.

gustatory	extirpate	autonomy	misanthrope
peripatetic	malevolent	chthonian	

1. The old _____, convinced that everyone he met had _____ intentions meant to harm him, relocated his home to a remote mountain cabin, far from the civilization he loathed. With the exception of his tools, clothing, rifle, and ammunition, he _____ every possible trace of the outside world from his cabin. Other than his _____ foraging in the wilderness for food or firewood, the hermit never again left the valley or visited the small town eight miles south of the cabin. In a short time, the hermit's _____ preferences changed from those of average, domestic meals to the tastes of nuts, berries, and wild game.

From the list below, supply the words needed to complete the paragraph. Some words will not be used.

puissance	scion	misanthrope	prominent
autonomy	supercilious	appellation	

2. After three years of working at the department store, Mark was the _____ candidate for the promotion to manager. He eagerly antici-pated the _____ that accompanied the position; there would be no more punch clocks and time cards, and no more _____ boss to belittle or second-guess Mark's decisions. Mark was certain that he had the _____ to work his way to the top of the company and eventually become a[n] _____ of the corporate dynasty.

From the list below, supply the words needed to complete the paragraph. Some words will not be used.

peripatetic	chthonian	puissance	coagulate
tutelary	jurisprudence	appellation	

3.   Audrey looked at an old photograph of her grandfather when he was a coal miner. Blackened with coal dust and squinting at the sun, grandfather looked like a[n] _____ creature emerging from his subterranean lair. Audrey, who knew her grandfather by the _____ "Papa," missed the wise old man's _____ guidance. Before Audrey enrolled in law school, she and her grandfather had often discussed the way in which _____ had changed from one generation to the next. In the days following the funeral, Audrey's fond memories seemed to _____ into a lump of sadness that weighed heavy in her being.

Exercise II

Sentence Completion

Complete the sentence in a way that shows you understand the meaning of the italicized vocabulary word.

1. The *supercilious* waiter didn't want to serve us because...

2. Gina thought that her neighbor was some kind of *misanthrope* because he...

3. It took weeks for Wendy to learn everyone's proper *appellation* after she accepted a job at...

4. When experiencing their first taste of *autonomy*, many young adults...

5. Millionaires with humble beginnings resented the *scions* of the railroad magnate because they...

6. During a secret meeting in the underground headquarters, the evil genius outlined his *malevolent* plan to...

7. The hot, melted candle wax will *coagulate* when...

8. Donald developed a *tutelary* relationship with his niece because...

9. Jane braved the snowstorm, but she didn't know if she would have the *puissance* to...

10. American *jurisprudence* prohibits a person from being permanently imprisoned without...

11. The ancient Greeks carved a *chthonian* deity into the prow of their warship in order to...

12. The explorer was surprised to find that the *gustatory* preferences of the natives were...

13. The dictator attempted to *extirpate* any dissidents from the ranks of his army by...

14. The witness easily identified the criminal when she saw his *prominent*...

15. Nancy preferred *peripatetic* vacations to...

Exercise III

Roots, Prefixes, and Suffixes

Study the entries and answer the questions that follow.

The roots *mit* and *miss* mean "send."
The root *duct* means "to lead."
The prefix *dis* means "away."
The prefix *ad* means "toward."
The prefix *ab* means "away from."
The prefix *in* means "into."
The prefix *trans* means "across."

1. *Using literal translations as guidance, define the following words without using a dictionary.*

    A. dismiss   D. abduct
    B. remit   E. induct
    C. admit   F. transmission

2. The prefix *per* means "through," so what does the word *permit* literally mean?

3. The prefix *de* means "from." If your process of reasoning leads you to an idea, you might call that idea a[n] _____.

4. An *emissary* is someone sent out to deliver a specific message, and a lamp _____, or "sends out" light. We can assume that the *e* prefix means _____.

5. Iron and copper are good _____ because they can be used to lead electrical current from one place to another.

6. What do you think the word *missile* literally means?

7. List as many words as you can think of that contain the prefix *trans*.

Exercise IV

Inference

Complete the sentences by inferring information about the italicized word from its context.

1. If you underestimate the *puissance* of your enemy, you might...

2. A *misanthrope* who avoids contact with people might not appreciate it if you...

3. If you fail to *extirpate* the bamboo shoots in your lawn, the plants might...

Exercise V

Writing

Here is a writing prompt similar to the one you will find on the writing portion of the ACT.

It is no secret that cigarette smoke is no good for you. Recent years have seen smoking bans *instituted* in bars, restaurants, and even public parks and sidewalks in some areas. As anti-tobacco groups continue to press governments to enact further bans, however, even nonsmokers are beginning to show signs of resistance, asking whether the bans are exceeding the primary purpose of protecting nonsmokers and instead are becoming a way to enforce the will of nonsmokers upon smokers. If smokers are hurting no one but themselves, then who has the right to make them stop?

Similarly, if it is acceptable to protect smokers from themselves, where do the bans end? Does alcohol get banned next? Processed sugar? Fried food? All these things have a deleterious effect on health. Neither do the bans need to end with food and drugs: many communities ban what they label as risky behavior, such as riding motorcycles without helmets, or not wearing seatbelts while driving cars.

Sometimes, bans are justified as necessary in order to save money for everyone by preventing situations requiring chronic medical care that cumulatively drive up the cost of health insurance. Is that the type of cost, though, that should be regulated on behalf of stakeholders? Does it intrude upon basic freedoms, or, specifically, everyone's right to the pursuit of happiness?

Is it good sense, or is it tyranny, to restrict freedom in order to protect people from themselves? Think of a ban on a food, drug, activity, or behavior that you feel is either vital to the community or entirely unnecessary. Write a letter to your local representative explaining your position. Your letter should identify the ban or proposed ban and present an argument as to whether or not the ban is a waste of taxpayer resources. Use examples, scenarios, experiences, or your own observations to support your argument.

Thesis: Write a one-sentence response to the above assignment. Make certain this single sentence offers a clear statement of your position.

Example: Motorcycle helmet laws are well intended, but laws that absolve people of responsibility for themselves are unrealistic demands for obedience by lawmakers.

_____

_____

Organizational Plan: If your thesis is the point on which you want to end, where does your essay need to begin? List the points of development that are inevitable in leading your reader from your beginning point to your end point. This list is your outline.

1. _____

2. _____

3. _____

Draft: Use your thesis as both your beginning and your end. Following your outline, write a good first draft of your essay. Remember to support all of your points with examples, facts, references to reading, etc.

Review and revise: Exchange essays with a classmate. Using the scoring guide for Sentence Formation and Variety on page 243, score your partner's essay (while he or she scores yours). Focus on the sentence structure and the use of language conventions. If necessary, rewrite your essay to improve the sentence structure and your use of language.

Exercise VI

English Practice

Improving Paragraphs
Read the following passage and then choose the best revision for the underlined portions of the paragraph. The questions will require you to make decisions regarding the revision of the reading selection. Some revisions are not of actual mistakes, but will improve the clarity of the writing.

The yawn—that irritating, ungainly, impolite disruption in board meetings, classrooms, <u>and in assembly</u>[1] lines all over the world—is but one of the great mysteries of humankind. Despite centuries of research, not one scientist can say with certainty why, exactly, people yawn. Oh, yes, they <u>theorize, lines</u>[2] of physiologists spout their suppositions: "Excessive carbon dioxide in the lungs!" "Under-stimulated brains!" "A primal response to ward off predators!" Unfortunately, while it would be fantastic if a simple yawn could frighten away a saber-toothed tiger, the real reason for yawning <u>is anyones guess</u>.[3]

1. A. NO CHANGE
   B. but in assembly
   C. and assembly
   D. with assembly

2. F. NO CHANGE
   G. theorize…lines
   H. theorize: lines
   J. theorize; lines

3. A. NO CHANGE
   B. is anyone's guess
   C. is anybodys guess
   D. is anyones' guess

People begin expressing their boredom very early in life—even before their born. The fact that fetuses yawn tells researchers that yawning is both involuntary and not due to a general lack of oxygen, since babies in utero do not breath oxygen as adults do. Now, simply determining why babies yawn has become a part of the quest to solve the riddle of yawns. <u>One theory that currently holds water is that yawning releases a chemical called surfactant, a substance that ensures that the alveoli, or tiny air pockets in the lungs, stay open.</u>[5] The production of surfactant is critical to development because it ensures that the lungs of a newborn will be ready to survive outside the womb; however, as everyone knows, the yawning continues well beyond birth.

4. Which choice best describes an error in the first sentence of paragraph 2?
    F. illogical relationship
    G. mixed metaphor
    H. incorrect possessive pronoun
    J. double negative

5. Which choice would improve the underlined sentence from paragraph 2?
    A. Rewrite the sentence to omit the cliché.
    B. Make two sentences out of the original sentence.
    C. Change *yawning* to *a yawn*.
    D. Place a semicolon after *surfactant*.

Boring classes, office meetings, lectures, seminars, and traffic jams take quite a toll on brains, and yawning does help to revive brains to better cope with the drudgery <u>to stay awake;</u>[6] however, yawning often strikes at seemingly arbitrary times. Stressful situations often beget yawns, as do colds, allergies, and sinus problems; even strenuous activity can spark excessive yawning. Experts agree that the lungs stretch during yawning, and the stretching prevents the collapse of tiny airways. This might help to explain why <u>yawning, that</u>[7] accompanies periods of shallow breathing, such as before and after sleeping, helps more air to enter the respiratory system. More air is good.

6. F. NO CHANGE
    G. to stay awake:
    H. for staying awake;
    J. of staying awake;

7. A. NO CHANGE
    B. yawning; that
    C. yawning—that
    D. yawning that

8. Which sentence should be deleted from paragraph 3?
    F. sentence 2
    G. sentence 3
    H. sentence 4
    J. sentence 5

The seemingly arbitrary nature of yawning has prompted many scientists to suggest that yawning is actually a form of involuntary communication. Human beings are creatures of imitation and quite receptive to suggestion; fifty-five percent of all people, in fact, will yawn within five minutes after seeing someone else yawn. Reading about yawns also has this effect, as well as <u>to talk about</u>[9] them and even thinking about them. Yawns also can express strong antisocial messages. Yawns are widely perceived as rude gestures. They frequently <u>infer</u>[10] boredom, but yawns often accompany feelings of rejection or even anger. Some medical professionals claim that yawning is stimulated by the same chemicals in the brain that affect emotions, moods, and appetites, so perhaps to ancient ancestors, yawns were involuntary, <u>visual signals that can be seen that alerted people</u>[11] that it was time to seek shelter for the night, which, therefore, synchronized sleeping patterns. Humans are, after all, social beings.

9. A. NO CHANGE
   B. talking about
   C. to talk of
   D. talk about

10. F. NO CHANGE
    G. interpret
    H. imply
    J. ensure

11. A. NO CHANGE
    B. visual signals, visible, that alerted people
    C. visual signals, which alerted people
    D. visual signals that alerted people

12. Correcting which error would fix the second sentence of paragraph 4?
    F. semicolon use
    G. use of *both*
    H. the hyphen in *fifty-five*
    J. *else* not possessive

Explaining yawning once and for all, perhaps someday scientists will find the proper combination of theories.[13] There seems to be a connection between prenatal yawns producing surfactant and adult yawns filling tiny airways in the lungs, but the ease with which humans will yawn simply because they saw someone else yawn suggests that the act is purely-psychosomatic.[14] Despite the many theories and facts pertaining to its origins, the mysterious act of yawning must join the tailbone and the appendix on the list of human anatomical conundrums.

13. A. NO CHANGE
    B. Perhaps someday scientists will, explaining yawning once and for all, find the proper combination of theories.
    C. Perhaps someday, scientists will find the proper combination of theories that explains yawning, once and for all.
    D. Explaining yawning, scientist will perhaps find the proper combination of theories, once and for all.

14. F. NO CHANGE
    G. purely, psychosomatic
    H. purely: psychosomatic
    J. purely psychosomatic

15. Which redundant sentence should be removed from paragraph 4?
    A. sentence 1
    B. sentence 2
    C. sentence 3
    D. sentence 5

Vocabulary
Power Plus
for the **ACT**
Vocabulary,
Reading, and Writing
Exercises for High Scores

Lesson Sixteen

1. **trenchant** (tren´ chənt) *adj.* effectively keen and forceful in thought or expression
The expert's *trenchant* comments silenced his critics.
syn: *cutting; forthright*   ant: *ambiguous; lenient; insipid*

2. **bourgeois** (bŏŏr zhwä´) *adj.* relating to the middle class
Adam hoped to become wealthy and abandon his *bourgeois* life.

3. **nascent** (nā´ sənt) *adj.* emerging; coming into existence
Jill attributed her *nascent* interest in sailing to her discovery of her seafaring ancestors.
syn: *blooming; fledgling*   ant: *dying; withering*

4. **indefeasible** (in di fē´ zə bəl) *adj.* not capable of being undone or voided
When times were rough, Teresa found comfort in the *indefeasible* love of her parents.
syn: *immutable; unremitting; constant*   ant: *varying; irregular; temporary*

5. **paladin** (pa´ lə dən) *n.* a heroic champion or leader
Though he was nothing more than a fictional cartoon character, Captain Justice was an inspiring *paladin* to children everywhere.
ant: *villain*

6. **sine qua non** (sin i kwä nän´) *n.* something essential; a prerequisite
Good communication is the *sine qua non* of a productive workplace.
syn: *must; requirement; necessity*   ant: *option*

7. **arcane** (är kān´) *adj.* known or understood by only a few; mysterious
The alchemist claimed to know an *arcane* formula for turning iron into gold.
syn: *secret; obscure; esoteric*   ant: *famous; obvious; exoteric*

8. **tangential** (tan jen´ shəl) *adj.* merely touching or slightly connected; digressing from the main point
The chairman asked the board to avoid *tangential* issues during the important meeting.
syn: *nonessential; peripheral*   ant: *vital; crucial; relevant*

9. **mercurial** (mər kyōōr´ ē əl) *adj.* quickly changing; volatile
    Frank acted like an entirely different person sometimes because of his
    mercurial personality.
    syn: fickle; unstable   *ant: unchanging; stable*

10. **exculpate** (ek´ skəl pāt) *v.* to clear of guilt; to declare innocent
    The judge dismissed the case when new evidence *exculpated* the
    defendant.
    syn: exonerate; acquit; vindicate   *ant: condemn; accuse; indict*

11. **salubrious** (sə lōō´ brē əs) *adj.* healthful
    Each day, after lunch, Tammy took a *salubrious* walk through the park.
    syn: salutary; wholesome   *ant: harmful; useless*

12. **vicissitude** (vi sis´ i tōōd) *n.* a sudden change or shift in one's life or
    circumstances
    She claimed that her many *vicissitudes* throughout life had made her a
    stronger person.
    syn: alteration; variation

13. **squelch** (skwelch) *v.* to suppress; squash
    The candidate desperately tried to *squelch* rumors that he had once been
    arrested.
    syn: extinguish; muffle; thwart   *ant: promote; support; enact*

14. **tyro** (tī´ rō) *n.* a beginner; novice
    Until he learned the trade, the *tyro* was advised to keep his ears open and
    his thoughts to himself.
    syn: amateur; neophyte; rookie   *ant: expert; master; guru*

15. **matriculate** (mə trik´ yə lāt) *v.* to admit or be admitted into a group
    or a college
    Sam's grades were high enough for him to *matriculate* at State in the fall.

Exercise I

Words in Context

From the list below, supply the words needed to complete the paragraph. Some words will not be used.

tyro	arcane	nascent	sine qua non
vicissitudes	matriculate	bourgeois	

1. Steve cannot complain about where the _____ of life led him. His excellent academic record allowed him to _____ into the university of his choice, and he now enjoys a[n] _____ lifestyle, despite having grown up in abject poverty. Now, Steve earns his living as an anthropologist studying the _____ data of lost civilizations, though recent finds have given him a[n] _____ interest in treasure hunting.

From the list below, supply the words needed to complete the paragraph. Some words will not be used.

vicissitudes	tangential	tyro	squelch
exculpate	trenchant	paladin	

2. Debbie had the _____ qualities of a good leader, but she was still a[n] _____ at charity work and never expected to become the _____ of her cause. It was true that she had always had _____ interests in eliminating poverty in underdeveloped nations, but until she realized how rewarding the work was, she had _____ any interests in making a career out of it.

From the list below, supply the words needed to complete the paragraph. Some words will not be used.

indefeasible	arcane	sine qua non	mercurial
exculpate	salubrious	bourgeois	

3. "An extra pair of socks is a[n] _____ in making it to the end of this hike," said Mr. Bronson, the wilderness guide. "Your feet will be your greatest asset when we're twenty miles from civilization, and you'll need to exercise _____ habits to keep them in good shape for the duration of the week. No excuse will _____ you if you run out of socks or if your boots are too tight." The group about to embark on a week-long, 120-mile hike understood the guide's concern; there were enough natural hazards to worry about, such as _____ weather and poisonous snakes, without complicating matters more by making _____ mistakes on the trail.

Exercise II

Sentence Completion

Complete the sentence in a way that shows you understand the meaning of the italicized vocabulary word.

1. A healthy breakfast is a *sine qua non* for...

2. The prestigious university refused to *matriculate* the student until...

3. The doctor told Phil to find a *salubrious* hobby that...

4. The old storyteller had such a *trenchant* way of speaking that...

5. To limit media interference during the investigation, the police *squelched*...

6. On some days, the *mercurial* teacher was pleasant and soft spoken, but...

7. According to the Declaration of Independence, life, liberty, and the pursuit of happiness are *indefeasible* rights that cannot...

8. Denny is a *tyro* at riding a bicycle, so he...

9. Despite experiencing the *vicissitudes* of life during the war, every member of the family...

10. The eccentric professor took pride in his *arcane* knowledge of...

11. After the court *exculpated* Jack of any wrongdoing, he...

12. The princess, detained high within the castle, hoped that someday a *paladin* would...

13. The reporter wanted a straight answer, but the public relations clerk gave only *tangential* statements that...

14. Our increasingly technological society must protect itself against *nascent* threats of...

15. Some people prefer a *bourgeois* life to a wealthy life because they do not...

Exercise III

Roots, Prefixes, and Suffixes

Study the entries and answer the questions that follow.

The roots *path* means "feel" or "suffer."
The root *pass* means "endure" or "suffer."
The prefix *in* means "not."
The prefix *syn* means "together with."
The prefix *com* means "together with."
The prefix *tele* means "across."
The prefix *a* means "not" or "none."
The suffix *ic* means "pertaining to."

1. *Using literal translations as guidance, define the following words without using a dictionary.*

   A. compassion D. telepathy
   B. impassive   E. apathy
   C. sympathy   F. passive

2. The prefix *en* means "in" or "into." What does the word *empathy* literally mean?

3. The word *pathetic* literally means _____.

4. *Passion* is another word for a strong _____.

5. List as many words as you can think of that contain the root *path*.

Exercise IV

Inference

Complete the sentences by inferring information about the italicized word from its context.

1. Tom's personality changed with each *vicissitude* he endured because he...

2. If you are still a *tyro* at swimming long distances, you might think twice about...

3. A *nascent* way of doing something will probably not become popular until...

Exercise V

Writing

Below is a reading passage followed by several multiple-choice questions similar to the ones you will encounter on the ACT. Carefully read the passage and choose the best answer for each of the questions.

The author of the following passage comments on the way in which technology influences the study of literature.

"Kids don't read enough" might sound like the anthem of any given English teacher, but suspend your bias for a few minutes and consider the facts. You might soon agree that television, movies, and other electronic media are, indeed, imperiling the critical thinking skills that only the study of literature affords.

5　　The average American child spends between 22 and 28 hours a week watching television; that's four hours a day, every day, and that exempts factors that might increase viewing, such as inclement weather. Four hours of television—this is the daily diet of the average American TV watcher. It's enough to be a part-time job! When you throw in all the other electronic media, such as movies, music, radio,

10　etc., the number climbs to a brain-rotting six hours a day; six hours and nothing to show for it.

As people vegetate for increasingly long periods each day, the popularity of reading, of course, lags. Children under eighteen spend, on average, less than one hour a day reading, and behold, reading assessment scores are plummeting!

15　Coincidence?

The insidiousness of television can be attributed to its many attractions—perpetual action, simple story lines, and neat endings that reinforce expectations of quick and complete gratification. Viewers can set their watches to the common narrative structures of most television shows: The show begins at 8:00 pm. At 8:05

20　the rising action has begun. A complication occurs at 8:15 and stymies the heroes until 8:20. The climax occurs at approximately 8:22, followed by a commercial break and then the denouement. It is not surprising that the young hedonists in the making find it difficult to progress through a substantial work of literature, whether it's a classic novel assigned in high school or a chapter book written for young

25　students. It is becoming dangerously routine for writers to cater to diminished attention spans by "dumbing down" literature, thus giving it the effect of television commercials or erratic web pages. Internet summaries of novels are replacing the actual stories; after all, the authors obviously didn't mean to include all that extra nonsense when they wrote the books.

30　Watching television, unlike reading, requires only a passive role from the viewer—imagination is unnecessary when all the imagery and ideas are already created for the audience; reading, however, is both a physical and a mental skill. The physical process—literally taking in the information—can be modeled at home and taught at both home and at school. The mental process by which readers internalize

35　and interpret literature must be developed one reader at a time, and it transcends the passive information gathering of television watching. Developing the tangential skills to understand texts—increased vocabulary, orthography, interpretation— takes practice, and that means more reading. These fundamental skills eventually coalesce into critical-thinking skills, and grant readers the ability to anticipate, 40 infer, and understand arguments and ideas in both texts and in any other form of communication.

Without the skills to interpret their own written language, people walk through a hazy world in which there are even fewer certainties than there are for people who do understand parts of it; they are like earthworms trying to understand the 45 cackling of birds—hungry birds, perhaps. The paragons of literature—those books, stories, and novels that have inspired great people to do great things—are simply unavailable to those who cannot read them. So please, turn off the television, even if it's for only one of the four nightly hours, and read something. Your brains will thank you one day.

1. The tone of the passage is best described as
    A. doubtful.
    B. animated.
    C. detached.
    D. troubled.

2. As used in line 6 of the passage, *exempts* most nearly means
    F. divides.
    G. accounts.
    H. excludes.
    J. determines.

3. The *hedonists* in paragraph 4 are people who
    A. learn quickly.
    B. seek pleasure.
    C. read profusely.
    D. debate television.

4. The simile in line 44 suggests that
    F. a lack of language skills can be dangerous.
    G. insects are higher-order animals than birds.
    H. mastering language skills is harder for some people than others.
    J. language skills are for those who want them.

5. Select the choice that best identifies the intended audience of the passage.
    A. teachers of English
    B. students of language
    C. administrators who make financial decisions
    D. parents of middle school students

6. The word *inclement* in line 7 most nearly means
    F. peaceful.
    G. unpredictable.
    H. humid.
    J. unpleasant.

7. The closest synonym for *transcends,* as it is used in line 35, is
    A. equals.
    B. challenges.
    C. surpasses.
    D. simulates.

8. The *denouement* mentioned in paragraph 4 probably refers to the part of a story in which
    F. the conflict is resolved and the characters return to normal.
    G. something occurs that changes the hero's task or makes it more difficult.
    H. the hero must win the challenge or suffer total failure.
    J. background information is provided for the characters.

9. Choose the best paraphrase of the following quotation (lines 42-45):

    "Without the skills to interpret their own written language, people walk through a hazy world in which there are even fewer certainties than there are for people who do understand parts of it; they are like earthworms trying to understand the cackling of birds—hungry birds, perhaps."

    A. Laziness is no excuse for poor reading comprehension.
    B. Everyone is most fluent in her or his own language, but it is hazardous to limit one's education.
    C. Trying to communicate with someone who cannot comprehend writing is like speaking a different language.
    D. An inability to understand language renders a person ignorant and prone to danger.

10. Lines 27-29 demonstrate the use of
    F. verbal irony, because the author means the opposite of what is written.
    G. personification, because the author gives literature human characteristics.
    H. foreshadowing, because the author predicts the decline of printed text.
    J. criticism, because the author suggests that most written content is unintentional nonsense.

Vocabulary
Power Plus
for the **ACT**
Vocabulary,
Reading, and Writing
Exercises for High Scores

Lesson Seventeen

1. **depravity** (di prav´ i tē) *n.* moral corruption; perversion
   Megan was shocked by the *depravity* occurring on the reputable college's
   campus.
   syn: immorality; debauchery; vice   *ant: virtue; goodness; decency*

2. **megalomania** (meg ə lō mā´ nē ə) *n.* having delusions of grandeur; an
   obsession with grandiose things
   Bill's actual-sized, wood reproduction of the Great Pyramid is said to be
   the result of the unemployed carpenter's *megalomania*.

3. **attribute** (ə trib´ yōōt) *v.* to relate to a particular cause; to ascribe
   Tim, partially deaf at twenty-one, *attributes* his hearing loss to his loud
   car stereo.
   syn: credit; blame; impute   *ant: dismiss; absolve*

4. **celerity** (sə ler´ i tē) *n.* swiftness of action; speed
   The factory lost money every second it was shut down, so the engineers
   worked with great *celerity* to repair the huge machine on the assembly
   line.
   syn: haste; rapidity; alacrity   *ant: delay; procrastination*

5. **alimentary** (a lə men´ tə rē) *adj.* pertaining to food, nutrition, or
   digestion
   The doctor questioned Missy about her *alimentary* habits when she
   complained of frequent indigestion.
   syn: dietary; nutritive

6. **congenital** (kən jen´ i təl) *adj.* dating from birth; inherent or natural
   The child's *congenital* heart condition was minor, but it had to be
   monitored for the rest of her life.
   syn: inborn; inherent   *ant: acquired; contracted*

7. **discourse** (dis´ kôrs) *n.* a discussion; a conversation
   The suspect refused to engage in any *discourse* about the crime until his
   lawyer arrived.
   syn: communication

8. **primordial** (prī môr´ dē əl) *adj.* first in time; original
    Long before the appearance of life, *primordial* Earth had a poisonous
    atmosphere and widespread volcanic activity.
    syn: primeval; prehistoric   *ant: recent; current*

9. **remuneration** (ri myōō nə rā´ shən) *n.* compensation; payment
    Clark demanded *remuneration* for having been brought to trial on false
    charges.
    syn: recompense; restitution; reimbursement

10. **attenuate** (ə ten´ ū āt) *v.* to reduce, weaken, or lessen
    The drought *attenuated* the flow of the mighty river until it was a mere stream.
    syn: diminish; shrink; reduce   *ant: strengthen; increase; intensify*

11. **mutable** (myōō´ tə bəl) *adj.* subject to change
    Pack an assortment of clothes, because the weather in the mountains is
    mutable.
    syn: variable; inconstant; unstable   *ant: consistent; constant; steady;*
    immutable

12. **ethereal** (i thēr´ ē əl) *adj.* light or airy; intangible; heavenly
    The subjects of Michelangelo's paintings often have an *ethereal* beauty.
    syn: celestial; impalpable; unearthly   *ant: heavy; thick; substantial*

13. **encomium** (en kō´ mē əm) *n.* formal praise; a tribute
    The publisher hoped that the author's first novel would receive an
    encomium from the demanding critic.
    syn: acclaim; endorsement; commendation   *ant: insult; condemnation*

14. **tactile** (tak´ təl) *adj.* pertaining to the sense of touch
    Roger still had *tactile* senses in his paralyzed legs, indicating that he had
    a good chance of walking again.

15. **ascetic** (ə set´ ik) *n.* a person who renounces material comforts and
    practices extreme self-denial
    The ancient fortune-teller was an *ascetic* who often abstained from food
    for days without complaint.

Exercise I

Words in Context

From the list below, supply the words needed to complete the paragraph. Some words will not be used.

attenuate	depravity	remuneration	primordial
encomiums	discourse	ethereal	

1.   Paige, a researcher who had earned the _____ of the pharmaceutical industry for her accomplishments, frequently traveled to the jungles of Peru in pursuit of a natural compound thought to _____ the torturous side effects of chemotherapy. The jungle fascinated Paige; its thick vegetation and enormous plants gave her a sense of what the _____ forests of Earth must have looked like when dinosaurs grazed on treetops and the ground rumbled with volcanic activity. In the evenings, Paige usually sat quietly at her camp and watched as the fog crept slowly down the verdant hills and settled in the valley, blanketing the old forest in a[n] _____ haze, like something out of a dream. To Paige, witnessing such natural beauty was ample _____ for her hard work.

From the list below, supply the words needed to complete the paragraph. Some words will not be used.

ethereal	ascetic	congenital	depravity
attribute	megalomania	mutable	

2.   During the new mayor's campaign, he claimed to be a political _____ with the goal of reducing all wasteful government spending and ending _____ within the ranks of the city government; however, the mayor's promises must have been _____ because his first action as mayor was to approve the construction of an unnecessary new park. Critics _____ the expensive project to the new mayor's _____, which was explained further when the mayor published his self-promoting autobiography.

From the list below, supply the words needed to complete the paragraph. Some words will not be used.

remuneration	celerity	alimentary	congenital
attribute	discourse	tactile	

3. All of Mike's _____ senses were still numbed after the surgery, but he was able to hear the _____ between his wife and the surgeon. The _____ stomach condition that had interfered with Mike's _____ processes since he was a baby had been corrected, and Mike would simply need plenty of rest to heal with _____.

Exercise II

Sentence Completion

Complete the sentence in a way that shows you understand the meaning of the italicized vocabulary word.

1. Kristen was awed by the *ethereal* sight of...

2. *Depravity* in the cult eventually caused...

3. *Discourse* among the students suddenly stopped when...

4. Dave, who frequently indulged in gourmet pleasures, called his wife an *ascetic* because she refused to...

5. The plans are *mutable*, so be prepared to...

6. Tim's *megalomania* makes life difficult for his friends because he is constantly...

7. The archaeologist found fossils of *primordial* microorganisms when she...

8. The safecracker wore gloves whenever he wasn't working so that his *tactile* senses would be sharp enough to...

9. *Celerity* of work was important to the construction crew because...

10. Lisa enjoyed the *encomium* from all the townspeople for...

11. After the recall, the automobile manufacturer said that *remunerations* would be provided for anyone who...

12. Logan *attributes* crop circles to UFOs, but most of his friends...

13. An earthworm's *alimentary* process is...

14. The high rate of *congenital* birth defects in the area was blamed on...

15. The rising costs of building supplies *attenuated* the couple's desire to...

Exercise III

Roots, Prefixes, and Suffixes

Study the entries and answer the questions that follow.

The roots *grad* and *gress* mean "step."
The roots *ced* and *cess* mean "go."
The prefix *de* means "down."
The prefix *pro* means "forward."
The prefix *re* means "back."
The prefix *di* means "apart" or "away from."
The prefix *trans* means "across" or "through."

1. *Using literal translations as guidance, define the following words without using a dictionary.*

    A. regression
    B. procession
    C. digress
    D. recede
    E. degrade
    F. progression

2. The prefix *se* means "away." In the 1860s, the Confederate States tried to _____ (literally, "go away") from the Union.

3. A synonym for *sin* that literally means "stepping across the line" is

    _____.

4. If the prefix *ex* means "outside," what does the word *exceed* literally mean?

5. List as many words as you can think of that contain the roots *ced* or *cess*.

6. List as many words as you can think of that contain the roots *grad* or *gress*.

Exercise IV

Inference

Complete the sentences by inferring information about the italicized word from its context.

1. The fire chief *attributed* the blaze to faulty wiring, so the police had no need to…

2. An *ascetic* who eats roots, sleeps on the floor, and drinks only water, would probably decline an invitation to…

3. If father refuses to partake in any further *discourse* on the subject, then he does not want to…

Exercise V

Writing

Here is a writing prompt similar to the one you will find on the writing portion of the ACT.

> With the exception of certain comic book archvillains, perhaps, no people who live on Earth want to destroy the environment in which they live. Not even the greediest chemical corporation shareholders or oil barons want to pollute and contaminate the world that their families will inherit. It is a silly premise, akin to claiming that soldiers desire the horrors of war, or that astronomers secretly wish for asteroid collisions.
>
> Unfortunately, for conservationists, food, land, and money are finite, owned resources. In matters of the environment, most people must make compromises. Sometimes, dumping solid waste into a river seems like an acceptable price to pay for a secure job that will reliably feed a family and put a roof over its head, especially in economically depressed nations. Global warming, which may or may not have catastrophic consequences in decades to come, is a small concern for the billions (not millions) of people who desperately need the stability provided by a fossil-fuel driven global economy. For those whose basic needs of food, water, and shelter are in demand, protecting the environment, by necessity, is a low priority.
>
> At the center of the environmental conflict is the amount of compromise that should be taking place. Should protection of the environment, including waterways, air quality, and threatened or endangered animals, have precedence over job creation? Should a factory which pollutes be allowed to operate, or continue operating, as

long as it pays the fines? Should machines be shut down and employees laid off if endangered animals are discovered in proximity to pollutants?

For this essay, put yourself in the role of someone who stands to either win or lose in the conflict between environment and economy. Take a position as to which side should dominate in the law. Be sure to account for newly rising industrial nations (some of which fester with water and air pollution) as much as you consider post-industrial nations such as the United States, where the conflict is often portrayed as a game of extremes—overzealous environmental activists who regard bird habitat as more important than hospital funding versus greedy corporations which willfully dodge pollution regulations in order to increase revenues.

Write your essay as a letter from one side of the debate (your side) to the opposition. Identify your position and support your argument using at least three supporting ideas.

Thesis: Write a one-sentence response to the above assignment. Make certain this sentence offers a clear statement of your position.

Example: Because the people who stand to profit will always push the limits of the law, environmental protection must always be enforced, even when it seems to oppose the survival of people who work in polluting industries.

_____

_____

Organizational Plan: If your thesis is the point on which you want to end, where does your essay need to begin? List the points of development that are inevitable in leading your reader from your beginning point to your end point. This list is your outline.

1. _____

2. _____

3. _____

Draft: Use your thesis as both your beginning and your end. Following your outline, write a good first draft of your essay. Remember to support all of your points with examples, facts, references to reading, etc.

Review and revise: Exchange essays with a classmate. Using the scoring guide for Word Choice on page 244, score your partner's essay (while he or she scores yours). Focus on word choice and the use of language conventions. If necessary, rewrite your essay to improve your word choice and your use of language.

Exercise VI

English Practice

Identifying Sentence Errors

Identify the errors in the following sentences. Choose the answer that fixes the error. If the sentence contains no error, select NO CHANGE.

1. We saved enough money from the previous <u>three month's paychecks</u>, and we can finally afford to go on a long vacation to Rome.
    A. NO CHANGE
    B. three months' paychecks
    C. three months paychecks
    D. three months paycheck's

2. Last April, members of the senior class took a trip from Buffalo to Niagara Falls, New York, and then across the border <u>of Toronto Canada</u>.
    F. NO CHANGE
    G. for Toronto, Canada
    H. at Toronto, Canada
    J. to Toronto, Canada

3. We visited Tom in the hospital after his car accident; <u>he seems good,</u> and the broken bones are almost completely healed.
    A. NO CHANGE
    B. he seems good,
    C. he seemed well,
    D. he seemed good:

4. <u>Although</u> the elderly King James died last week after a long illness, his son will legally become the new ruler of the country.
    F. NO CHANGE
    G. While
    H. However
    J. Because

5. <u>Jeremy, the person with whom I've been carpooling, his car broke down yesterday.</u>
    A. NO CHANGE
    B. Jeremy's car broke down yesterday. He was the person with whom I carpool.
    C. I had been carpooling with Jeremy, but his car broke down yesterday.
    D. I've carpooled with Jeremy; yesterday, his car broke down.

Improving Sentences

The underlined portion of each sentence below contains some flaw. Select the answer that best corrects the flaw.

6.   Neither Charlotte nor her sisters is going to the mall.
     F. Neither Charlotte or her sisters is going to the mall.
     G. Neither Charlotte nor her sisters are going to the mall.
     H. Neither her sisters nor Charlotte are going to the mall.
     J. Neither Charlotte and her sister are going to the mall.

7.   The assistance of two electricians, one network administrator, an informa-
     tion technology specialist, and three helpers were necessary to fix all the
     computer errors that had caused the crash.
     A. was necessary to fix all the computer errors that had caused the crash.
     B. were necessary to fix the computer errors that caused the crash.
     C. were necessary to fix all the computer errors, which had caused the
         crash.
     D. was necessary to fix all the computer errors that crashed.

8.   One thing I know that will keep me from traveling abroad, and those are
     the high costs of flying.
     F. I know one thing that will keep me from traveling abroad—the high
         cost of flying.
     G. One thing that I know that will keep me from traveling overseas, are
         the high costs of flying.
     H. I know one thing keeping me from traveling abroad, and that is the
         risks of flying.
     J. Traveling abroad and the high costs of flying will keep me from
         doing these things, I know that.

9.   He is as strong, if not stronger than his father.
     A. He is as strong, if not stronger then his father was.
     B. He is as strong, if not more strong than his father.
     C. He is as strong as, if not stronger then his father.
     D. He is as strong as his father, if not stronger.

10. An aspiring pianist should spend hours practicing; otherwise you will
     never be successful.
     F. practicing because otherwise, you will never be successful.
     G. practicing; otherwise, he or she will never be successful.
     H. in practicing; otherwise, you will never be a success.
     J. practicing, or else you will never be successful.

Vocabulary
Power Plus
for the **ACT**
Vocabulary,
Reading, and Writing
Exercises for High Scores

Lesson Eighteen

1. **poignant** (poin´ yənt) *adj.* very moving; touching
The movie would be simply mediocre if it didn't contain an especially *poignant* scene.
syn: emotional; affecting; sentimental   *ant: unemotional; cold*

2. **venial** (vē´ nē əl) *adj.* easily excused or forgiven
A *venial* offense such as jaywalking usually bears little or no fine.
syn: pardonable; remittable; excusable   *ant: inexcusable; unforgivable*

3. **satiate** (sā´ shē āt) *v.* to satisfy fully
No amount of riches could *satiate* the greedy baron.
syn: gratify; suit

4. **vituperative** (vī tōō´ pə rə tiv) *adj.* fault-finding; verbally abusive
The *vituperative* drill instructor screamed at the new recruit for not having shiny boots and a pressed uniform.
syn: castigating; derisive; scathing   *ant: flattering; sweet; kind*

5. **cumulative** (kyōō´ myə lə tiv) *adj.* resulting from accumulation; increasing
Her *cumulative* grade point average, from the ninth grade to the present, is 3.7.
syn: aggregate; summative; collective   *ant: decreasing; subtracting*

6. **exhilaration** (ig zil´ ə rā´ shən) *n.* thrill; invigoration
A sense of *exhilaration* overwhelmed me as I reached the summit and looked down at the forest far below.
syn: excitement; elation   *ant: boredom; apathy; ennui*

7. **pundit** (pun´ dit) *n.* a critic
The political *pundit* commented on government actions each morning on a radio show.
syn: commentator; reviewer; analyzer

8. **propriety** (prə prī´ i tē) *n.* proper behavior; appropriateness
The man carried himself with such *propriety* that few would have guessed he was homeless.
syn: decency; etiquette; seemliness   *ant: rudeness; indecency*

9. **goad** (gōd) *v.* to urge forward; to prod
The kids in the schoolyard *goaded* the boy into sticking his tongue to the frozen flagpole.
syn: spur; press; incite   *ant: deter; discourage; dissuade*

10. **impunity** (im pyōō´ ni tē) *n.* freedom from punishment, penalty, or harm
No one can speak against the king with *impunity*.
syn: immunity; liberty   *ant: vulnerability; risk*

11. **surfeit** (sûr´ fit) *n.* an excessive amount
A *surfeit* of oranges this year drove the price down.
syn: excess; overabundance; surplus   *ant: shortage; dearth; deficiency*

12. **trite** (trīt) *adj.* overused; hackneyed; clichéd
I could tell by my agent's *trite* reply that she hadn't actually read my manuscript.
syn: banal; routine; timeworn   *ant: fresh; provocative; original*

13. **extricate** (ek´ stri kāt) *v.* to release; to disentangle
The escape artist *extricated* himself from the chains holding him under water in less than one minute.
syn: free; deliver; liberate   *ant: entangle; hinder*

14. **superfluous** (sōō pûr´ flōō əs) *adj.* unnecessary; excessive
The new luxury SUV had many *superfluous* options, including two televisions.
syn: exorbitant; gratuitous; extravagant   *ant: essential; necessary; imperative*

15. **lithe** (līth) *adj.* graceful in motion; moving and bending with ease
The *lithe* gymnast's movements were graceful and seemingly effortless.
syn: agile; flowing; supple   *ant: rigid; clumsy; awkward*

Exercise I

Words in Context

From the list below, supply the words needed to complete the paragraph. Some words will not be used.

surfeit	lithe	superfluous	satiate
pundit	trite	vituperative	goad

1. The author knew that his novel was far from great, but according to the _____ reviews of numerous _____, the book was simply awful. Most critics noted that the detective thriller contains a[n] _____ of _____ expressions that could have been stolen from the script of any low-budget action film, and that the author used little creativity in allowing the hero of the novel, Lance Driver, to solve most of his problems through the use of _____ violence. No one would ever _____ him into writing another mystery.

From the list below, supply the words needed to complete the paragraph. Some words will not be used.

extricate	pundit	venial	exhilaration
poignant	goad	lithe	

2. Two months after the tragic bridge collapse, the lone survivor told her _____ survival tale to a newspaper reporter. Sharon had been wounded when the roadway surface of the bridge fell more than sixty feet to the water, but luckily she was _____ enough to _____ herself from the mangled wreckage of the bridge and her car. Feeling the pain of multiple fractures, Sharon crawled up a fallen steel girder. She recalls the _____ she felt when she first saw the rescue helicopter approaching; however, the feeling was short-lived because Sharon quickly passed out from shock.

From the list below, supply the words needed to complete the paragraph. Some words will not be used.

vituperative	cumulative	impunity	satiate
propriety	exhilaration	venial	

3.   To Randy's parents, wasting hard-earned money was no _____ crime. When Randy was six years old, his parents opened a savings account for him. Over the years, the _____ balance rose to the thousands of dollars, but Randy could not touch it unless he proved that he would demonstrate _____ in handling the money. On occasion, Randy was allowed to use some of it to _____ his need to increase the size of his baseball card collection, but he was certainly never allowed to go to the mall and spend with _____; the money was meant to pay for college, after all.

Exercise II

Sentence Completion

Complete the sentence in a way that shows you understand the meaning of the italicized vocabulary word.

1.   Each morning, the *pundit* scanned the newspaper to find...

2.   Every time Roslyn watches that *poignant* black-and-white movie, she...

3.   Frank harvested a *surfeit* of tomatoes from his garden this year, so he...

4.   Cal stopped allowing his dog to run free in the woods after he had to *extricate* the animal from...

5.   The mobsters operated the illegal casino with *impunity* until...

6.   When a bowling ball fell on Dad's foot after he opened the closet, he broke into a series of *vituperative* screams about...

7.   Shannon had to avoid any *superfluous* expenses until she...

8   The new supervisor didn't mind if workers committed *venial* errors, but if when they began to make mistakes that cost the company money, she...

9.   The cover of the greeting card featured a *trite* expression about...

10. Before the field trip, the teacher warned the students that anyone who fails to represent the school with *propriety* would…

11. Ben didn't eat enough to *satiate* himself because he didn't want to…

12. Brad lived for experiencing the *exhilaration* of…

13. After twenty years of working with uranium, Steve's *cumulative* radiation exposure finally…

14. The crowd stared at the almost hypnotic movements of the *lithe*…

15. Craig had never been swimming, so his parents had to *goad* him to…

Exercise III

Roots, Prefixes, and Suffixes

Study the entries and answer the questions that follow.

The roots *ag* and *act* mean "to do" or "drive."
The roots *mov* and *mot* mean "to move."
The prefix *de* means "down."
The prefix *in* means "not."
The prefix *pro* means "forward."

1. Using literal translations as guidance, define the following words without using a dictionary.

   A. promote   D. proactive
   B. inactive   E. immovable
   C. demote   F. agitate

2. The prefix *com* means "together." What does the word *commotion* literally mean?

3. If a story *moves* you, then it might cause you to experience a particular _____, or feeling.

4. *Mob* is another form of the root *mov*. List as many words as you can think of that contain the root *mob*.

5. List as many words as you can think of that contain the roots *mov* or *mot*.

Exercise IV

Inference

Complete the sentences by inferring information about the italicized word from its context.

1. A teacher might overlook a student's *venial* faults if the student...

2. If the fishermen have to *extricate* a dolphin from the fishing net, then the dolphin must be...

3. Ambassadors must demonstrate great *propriety* while meeting with foreign officials because...

Exercise V

Critical Reading

Below is a reading passage followed by several multiple-choice questions similar to the ones you will encounter on the ACT. Carefully read the passage and choose the best answer for each of the questions.

The following passage is an excerpt from Jane Eyre, *by Charlotte Brontë (1816–1855).*

Ere the half-hour ended, five o'clock struck; school was dismissed, and all were gone into the refectory to tea. I now ventured to descend: it was deep dusk; I retired into a corner and sat down on the floor. The spell by which I had been so far supported began to dissolve; reaction took place, and soon, so overwhelming was
5 the grief that seized me, I sank prostrate with my face to the ground. Now I wept: Helen Burns was not here; nothing sustained me; left to myself I abandoned myself, and my tears watered the boards. I had meant to be so good, and to do so much at Lowood: to make so many friends, to earn respect and win affection. Already I had made visible progress: that very morning I had reached the head of my class;
10 Miss Miller had praised me warmly; Miss Temple had smiled approbation; she had promised to teach me drawing, and to let me learn French, if I continued to make similar improvement two months longer: and then I was well received by my fellow-pupils; treated as an equal by those of my own age, and not molested by any; now, here I lay again crushed and trodden on; and could I ever rise more?
15 "Never," I thought; and ardently I wished to die. While sobbing out this wish in broken accents, some one approached: I started up—again Helen Burns was near me; the fading fires just showed her coming up the long, vacant room; she brought my coffee and bread.

"Come, eat something," she said; but I put both away from me, feeling as if a
20 drop or a crumb would have choked me in my present condition. Helen regarded
me, probably with surprise: I could not now abate my agitation, though I tried hard;
I continued to weep aloud. She sat down on the ground near me, embraced her
knees with her arms, and rested her head upon them; in that attitude she remained
silent as an Indian. I was the first who spoke.
25 "Helen, why do you stay with a girl whom everybody believes to be a liar?"
"Everybody, Jane? Why, there are only eighty people who have heard you called so,
and the world contains hundreds of millions."
"But what have I to do with millions? The eighty, I know, despise me."
"Jane, you are mistaken: probably not one in the school either despises or
30 dislikes you: many, I am sure, pity you much."
"How can they pity me after what Mr. Brocklehurst has said?"
"Mr. Brocklehurst is not a god: nor is he even a great and admired man: he is little
liked here; he never took steps to make himself liked. Had he treated you as an
especial favorite, you would have found enemies, declared or covert, all around you; as
35 it is, the greater number would offer you sympathy if they dared. Teachers and pupils
may look coldly on you for a day or two, but friendly feelings are -concealed in their
hearts; and if you persevere in doing well, these feelings will ere long appear so much
the more evidently for their temporary suppression. Besides, Jane"—she paused.
"Well, Helen?" said I, putting my hand into hers: she chafed my fingers gently
40 to warm them, and went on.
"If all the world hated you, and believed you wicked, while your own conscience
approved you, and absolved you from guilt, you would not be without friends."
"No; I know I should think well of myself; but that is not enough: if others don't
love me I would rather die than live—I cannot bear to be solitary and hated, Helen.
45 Look here; to gain some real affection from you, or Miss Temple, or any other whom
I truly love, I would willingly submit to have the bone of my arm broken, or to let a
bull toss me, or to stand behind a kicking horse, and let it dash its hoof at my chest—"
"Hush, Jane! You think too much of the love of human beings; you are too
impulsive, too vehement; the sovereign hand that created your frame, and put life
50 into it, has provided you with other resources than your feeble self, or than creatures
feeble as you. Besides this earth, and besides the race of men, there is an invisible
world and a kingdom of spirits: that world is round us, for it is everywhere; and
those spirits watch us, for they are commissioned to guard us; and if we were dying
in pain and shame, if scorn smote us on all sides, and hatred crushed us, angels see
55 our tortures, recognize our innocence (if innocent we be: as I know you are of this
charge which Mr. Brocklehurst has weakly and pompously repeated at second-hand
from Mrs. Reed; for I read a sincere nature in your ardent eyes and on your clear
front), and God waits only the separation of spirit from flesh to crown us with a full
reward. Why, then, should we ever sink overwhelmed with distress, when life is so
60 soon over, and death is so certain an entrance to happiness—to glory?"
I was silent; Helen had calmed me; but in the tranquility she imparted there was
an alloy of inexpressible sadness. I felt the impression of woe as she spoke, but I
could not tell whence it came; and when, having done speaking, she breathed a little
fast and coughed a short cough, I momentarily forgot my own sorrows to yield to a
65 vague concern for her.
Resting my head on Helen's shoulder, I put my arms round her waist; she drew
me to her, and we reposed in silence. We had not sat long thus, when another

person came in. Some heavy clouds, swept from the sky by a rising wind, had left the moon bare; and her light, streaming in through a window near, shone full both
70   on us and on the approaching figure, which we at once recognized as Miss Temple.

"I came on purpose to find you, Jane Eyre," said she; "I want you in my room; and as Helen Burns is with you, she may come too."

We went; following the superintendent's guidance, we had to thread some intricate passages, and mount a staircase before we reached her apartment; it
75   contained a good fire, and looked cheerful. Miss Temple told Helen Burns to be seated in a low armchair on one side of the hearth, and herself taking another, she called me to her side.

"Is it all over?" she asked, looking down at my face. "Have you cried your grief away?"
80   "I am afraid I never shall do that."

"Why?"

"Because I have been wrongly accused; and you, ma'am, and everybody else, will now think me wicked."

"We shall think you what you prove yourself to be, my child. Continue to act
85   as a good girl, and you will satisfy us."

"Shall I, Miss Temple?"

"You will," said she, passing her arm round me. "And now tell me who is the lady whom Mr. Brocklehurst called your benefactress?"

"Mrs. Reed, my uncle's wife. My uncle is dead, and he left me to her care."
90   "Did she not, then, adopt you of her own accord?"

"No, ma'am; she was sorry to have to do it: but my uncle, as I have often heard the servants say, got her to promise before he died that she would always keep me."

"Well now, Jane, you know, or at least I will tell you, that when a criminal is accused, he is always allowed to speak in his own defense. You have been charged
95   with falsehood; defend yourself to me as well as you can. Say whatever your memory suggests is true; but add nothing and exaggerate nothing."

I resolved, in the depth of my heart, that I would be most moderate—most correct; and, having reflected a few minutes in order to arrange coherently what I had to say, I told her all the story of my sad childhood. Exhausted by emotion, my
100 language was more subdued than it generally was when it developed that sad theme; and mindful of Helen's warnings against the indulgence of resentment, I infused into the narrative far less of gall and wormwood than ordinary. Thus restrained and simplified, it sounded more credible: I felt as I went on that Miss Temple fully believed me.
105   In the course of the tale I had mentioned Mr. Lloyd as having come to see me after the fit: for I never forgot the, to me, frightful episode of the red-room: in detailing which, my excitement was sure, in some degree, to break bounds; for nothing could soften in my recollection the spasm of agony which clutched my heart when Mrs. Reed spurned my wild supplication for pardon, and locked me a
110 second time in the dark and haunted chamber.

I had finished: Miss Temple regarded me a few minutes in silence; she then said, "I know something of Mr. Lloyd; I shall write to him; if his reply agrees with your statement, you shall be publicly cleared from every imputation; to me, Jane, you are clear now."

1. The narrator of this passage is
    A. Jane, a school-aged girl
    B. Mrs. Reed, Jane's aunt.
    C. Helen, a student.
    D. Mr. Brocklehurst, the schoolmaster.

2. Helen Burns is probably
    F. Jane's sister.
    G. Jane's guidance counselor.
    H. Jane's friend.
    J. Jane's English teacher.

3. Helen warns Jane about befriending Mr. Brocklehurst because
    A. Mr. Brocklehurst is the superintendent.
    B. it would cause people to dislike Jane.
    C. Mr. Brocklehurst does not like Helen.
    D. he is an acquaintance of Jane's family.

4. According to the passage, Jane was
    F. caught in a lie.
    G. playing in the classroom and got into a fight.
    H. accused of something that she did not do.
    J. accused of something that Helen did.

5. Which statement best demonstrates the intended idea of the following quotation?

    > "If all the world hated you, and believed you wicked, while your own conscience approved you, and absolved you from guilt, you would not be without friends."

    A. Friends will always believe you, as long as you believe yourself.
    B. No one needs friends.
    C. You always have a friend in yourself.
    D. Only what you think is important, unless you think yourself to be guilty.

6. As used in line 62, *alloy* most nearly means
    F. binary number.
    G. blending.
    H. metal.
    J. contaminant.

7. Which choice best paraphrases the following quotation?

   "...mindful of Helen's warnings against the indulgence of resentment,
   I infused into the narrative far less of gall and wormwood than
   ordinary."

   A. Being mindful of Helen's warning about spite, I focused on positive
      things during my explanation.
   B. The resentment that I had for Helen did not stop me from infusing
      the ordinary nerve into my story.
   C. Heeding Helen's warning about being resentful, I made my account
      less spiteful than it might have typically been.
   D. Helen's warning about resentment allowed me to be polite, as usual,
      during my narrative.

8. The story in this passage takes place
   F. at lunchtime, while Jane and Helen are waiting for their next class.
   G. in the early afternoon, before Mr. Brocklehurst returns from vacation.
   H. at night, after school has let out for the day.
   J. on Saturday, while Jane is in detention for lying on Friday.

9. This passage would likely be found in
   A. a newspaper column.
   B. a book report.
   C. a novel.
   D. a history textbook.

10. The most appropriate title for this passage would be
    F. A Day at School.
    G. Worry Not, Jane.
    H. Being the New Girl.
    J. Miss Temple's Mistake.

Vocabulary
Power Plus
for the ACT
Vocabulary,
Reading, and Writing
Exercises for High Scores

Lesson Nineteen

1. **stentorian** (sten tôr´ ē ən) *adj.* extremely loud
The lieutenant repeated the general's orders in a *stentorian* voice that could be heard by the entire regiment.
syn: blaring; booming; roaring   *ant: quiet; muted*

2. **propitious** (prō pish´ əs) *adj.* promising; auspicious
The gold doubloon was a *propitious* discovery for the explorers because it meant that the treasure was nearby.
syn: favorable; advantageous; beneficial   *ant: ominous; harmful; unfortunate*

3. **transient** (tran´ zē ənt) *adj.* remaining only a short time
The restaurant owner treated the regular customers better than she did the *transient* customers, who probably wouldn't return.
syn: temporary; fleeting; provisional   *ant: permanent; enduring*

4. **tremulous** (trem´ yə ləs) *adj.* timid; fearful
Afraid of being rejected, he asked her for a date in a *tremulous* voice.
syn: anxious; sheepish; nervous   *ant: brave; confident; bold*

5. **fulsome** (fŏŏl´ səm) *adj.* offensively flattering; insincere
The driver smirked and made a *fulsome* compliment to his opponent before the race.
syn: unctuous; ingratiating; fawning   *ant: sincere; heartfelt*

6. **utilitarian** (yōō til ə târ´ ē ən) *adj.* useful; practical
The hermit's *utilitarian* cabin provided shelter from the weather and a place to store food, but little else.
syn: practical; functional   *ant: useless*

7. **schism** (siz´ əm) *n.* a separation or division
The political party experienced a severe *schism* when members disagreed about how best to distribute the funds.
syn: break; estrangement; split   *ant: unification; merger; alliance*

8. **rescind** (ri sind´) *v.* to repeal; to make void
Congress was forced to *rescind* the unconstitutional law.
syn: recall; repeal; nullify   *ant: adopt; enact; promote*

9. **extant** (ek´ stənt) *adj.* still in existence
Despite the effectiveness of modern medicine, home remedies and the use of healing herbs are still *extant*.
syn: existent; present; remaining   *ant: extinct; dead; gone*

10. **inchoate** (in kō´ it) *adj.* not yet complete; undeveloped
He thought that with a little refining, his *inchoate* idea could easily become the invention of the century.
syn: rudimentary; preliminary; unformed   *ant: refined; shaped; developed*

11. **unwieldy** (un wēl´ dē) *adj.* not easily carried because of size, shape, or complexity
It took an hour to carry the *unwieldy* couch up the stairs to the apartment.
syn: awkward; cumbersome; ungainly   *ant: convenient; manageable*

12. **spurious** (spyŭr´ ē əs) *adj.* possible but ultimately false; not genuine
The evidence did not comply with the defendant's *spurious* testimony.
syn: counterfeit; bogus   *ant: legitimate; genuine; authentic*

13. **abjure** (ab jŭr´) *v.* to renounce or recant
During a public rally, the dictator forced the writer to *abjure* his criticism of the government.
syn: retract; revoke   *ant: assert; maintain; endorse*

14. **inveterate** (in vet´ ər it) *adj.* habitual; continuing
The *inveterate* criminal didn't retire until he was incarcerated.
syn: chronic

15. **dissipate** (dis´ ə pāt) *v.* to waste recklessly; to exhaust
It took only one month for the irresponsible son to *dissipate* his inheritance.
syn: squander; misuse   *ant: save; conserve*

Exercise I

Words in Context

From the list below, supply the words needed to complete the paragraph. Some words will not be used.

dissipate	inchoate	propitious	rescind
extant	transient	unwieldy	

1.   The tropical storm struck with swift fury; a rogue wave had destroyed the tiny ship's wheelhouse and pulled both the skipper and the first mate overboard into the raging sea. The engine and radio had been rendered inoperable, and the only _____ supplies consisted of a single case of bottled water and a small cooler containing sandwiches.

"We don't know how long we'll be adrift, so we cannot foolishly _____ our limited food supply," said Nancy, as the passengers stared horrified at the broken glass lying on the deck where the wheelhouse once stood. Jack, who at least had a[n] _____ knowledge of mechanics, fiddled with the engine in an attempt to get it to run. That night, passengers helplessly watched the _____ lights of ships passing in the distance, but had no means of signaling them. Early the next morning, passengers awoke to the _____ sound of the ship's engine sputtering and then, miraculously, running.

From the list below, supply the words needed to complete the paragraph. Some words will not be used.

dissipate	spurious	unwieldy	schism
inveterate	abjure	stentorian	

2.   Bill and Ted had been friends for twenty years, until falling in love with the same woman caused a[n] _____ that drove them apart. Though the woman had no interest in either of the men and had long ago departed the small town, a[n] _____ contempt remained between the former pals for years. When they inadvertently crossed paths with one another around town or at the grocery store, Bill and Ted exchanged _____ greetings that did little to hide their mutual scorn. It took twelve years for the two men to _____ their dislike for each other and cast off the _____ grudge that had burdened them throughout their lives.

From the list below, supply the words needed to complete the paragraph. Some words will not be used.

rescind	extant	fulsome	stentorian
utilitarian	tremulous	schism	

3. Ryan was just about to doze off when a[n] _____ announcement blasted over the intercom, causing some of the more _____ passengers to sit up straight in their coach-class seats. In his most _____ voice, the captain thanked the passengers for flying the airline and then _____ his previous estimate that the flight would be late; passengers could expect to arrive in Anchorage in less than one hour. The news pleased Ryan; if the flight arrived early, he would have ample time to prepare for his important business meeting. He smiled as he slipped his notebook computer into a[n] _____ leather briefcase and buckled his seatbelt.

Exercise II

Sentence Completion

Complete the sentence in a way that shows you understand the meaning of the italicized vocabulary word.

1. Phil had only *transient* exposure to the contagious patients, so he didn't worry about…

2. Jill wants a *utilitarian* family car, but her husband wants…

3. The campers could not *dissipate* their supplies because they…

4. Vicky replaced her *unwieldy* purse with one that…

5. When a *schism* resulted over the best way to find the trail, half of the lost hikers…

6. The angry teacher made a *stentorian* request for the students to…

7. During the questioning, the captured soldier created a *spurious* story that…

8. The corporation hired a lobbyist to convince the government to *rescind* legislation that…

9. To the crew of the marooned ship, a bird carrying nesting materials was a *propitious* sign that...

10. When new discoveries proved him wrong, the scientist was driven to *abjure*...

11. Mike, an *inveterate* joker, constantly thinks about...

12. The *tremulous* man could not bring himself to...

13. The novel will remain *inchoate* until the author...

14. The boss hated hearing the *fulsome* comments of employees who were simply trying to...

15. The supports of the century-old railroad bridge are still *extant*, despite...

Exercise III

Roots, Prefixes, and Suffixes

Study the entries and answer the questions that follow.

The root *mis* means "hatred."
The root *bio* means "life."
The root *morph* means "shape."
The root *anthrop* means "human."
The suffix *logy* means "study of."
The prefix *meta* means "change."
The prefix *anti* means "against."
The prefix *a* means "not" or "none."

1. Using literal translations as guidance, define the following words without using a dictionary.

A. anthropomorphic   D. antibiotic
B. metamorphosis   E. biology
C. anthropology   F. amorphous

2. The root *graph* means "writing." What does the word *biography* literally mean?

3. There is a special branch of linguistics (the study of language) called *morphology*. Explain the probable purpose of this branch.

4. A[n] _____ has a hatred for his or her fellow human beings.

5. List as many words as you can think of that contain the root *bio*.

Exercise IV

Inference

Complete the sentences by inferring information about the italicized word from its context.

1. Someone who has an *inchoate* understanding of electricity should not...

2. Your present jacket might look nice on you in the Arctic, but you'll need to replace it with a *utilitarian* coat that...

3. To get the *unwieldy* box from the store to your home, you might need to...

Exercise V

Writing

Here is a writing prompt similar to the one you will find on the writing portion of the ACT.

> Even during the economic recession toward the end of the first decade of the millennium, the amount of money the United States doled out to foreign nations increased to over $43 billion annually. This increase occurred against a setting of rising unemployment rates, a floundering housing market, heavy US military spending, and declining US manufacturing.
>
> Is it rational to send the money of US taxpayers abroad to assist other nations while unemployed US citizens barely manage to pay mortgages or buy groceries? Should we be helping other nations become more economically competitive while US schools, plagued with decreasing performance, are forced to cut academic budgets and school programs?
>
> Take a position on whether or not the taxes you pay should be spent for the improvement of foreign nations. Before you

decide, consider the benefits of foreign assistance in addition to the detriments; foreign assistance, ideally, is intended to be an investment. Investing in developing nations has the potential to yield economic allies and trading partners. Assisting young governments can prevent political instability and subsequent wars, which are always costly for anyone involved.

Imagine that you have been elected to the office of US Senator, and that you have been appointed to the Senate Foreign Relations Committee. You have an opportunity to reform US foreign assistance, but you will need to explain your recommendation. Identify where you stand on the issue and argue for or against increasing foreign spending. Support your argument using at least one example, experience, or observation.

Thesis: Write a one-sentence response to the above assignment. Make certain this single sentence offers a clear statement of your position.

Example: Foreign assistance is necessary to the development of young nations, which in turn, will create a better world and global economy.

_____

_____

Organizational Plan: If your thesis is the point on which you want to end, where does your essay need to begin? List the points of development that are inevitable in leading your reader from your beginning point to your end point. This list is your outline.

1. _____

2. _____

3. _____

Draft: Use your thesis as both your beginning and your end. Following your outline, write a good first draft of your essay. Remember to support all of your points with examples, facts, references to reading, etc.

Review and revise: Exchange essays with a classmate. Using the Holistic scoring guide on page 245, score your partner's essay (while he or she scores yours). If necessary, rewrite your essay to correct the problems indicated by the essay's score.

Exercise VI

English Practice

Improving Paragraphs
Read the following passage and then choose the best revision for the underlined portions of the paragraph. The questions will require you to make decisions regarding the revision of the reading selection. Some revisions are not of actual mistakes, but will improve the clarity of the writing.

(1) Any day of the week, between 10:00 am to 11 pm, drop by a major bookstore. (2) You will see why movies and television will never replace written <u>literature, people</u>[2] simply love to hold a book. (3) They find excitement, comfort, <u>an adventure, and</u>[3] familiarity in both handling and reading books.

1. Which choice best corrects an error in sentence 1?
   A. remove the comma after *week*
   B. remove the comma after *eleven pm*
   C. replace *drop* with *stop*
   D. replace *to* with *and*

2. F. NO CHANGE
   G. literature: people
   H. literature people
   J. literature because people

3. A. NO CHANGE
   B. adventure. And
   C. adventure, and
   D. an adventure and

(4) Holding a book transports the reader to earlier times, even to the happiness of childhood, when we snuggled up for that last story before bedtime. (5) Bedtime stories taught us to associate the closeness of a parent, the safety of home, and the joy of a story; on the contrary, some remnant of this satisfaction carries over to our more mature encounters with books. (6) The physicality of those experiences is somehow enclosed within the covers of every new book we touch.

4. In sentence 5, *on the contrary* should be replaced with
   F. indeed
   G. even so
   H. after all
   J. in simpler terms

(7) Even the smell of a book is captivating. (8) The smell of a book of photographs takes us back to the time when we <u>poured over</u>[5] pictures, trying to imagine the motion of Willie Mays making "The Catch," or searching the faces of soldiers to understand their feelings before they landed on the <u>beaches of normandy</u>.[6] (9) The pulp-smell of an old book can bring back the memories of discovering classics like *Jane Eyre, Wuthering Heights,* or *Pride and <u>Prejudice books</u>*[7] that carried us through long summers at a grandmother's house. (10) The same smell, though, reminds us of finally being forced to open up a copy of David Copperfield to fulfill a summer reading list assingment, so it is not always a good experience. (11) Connecting books with smell is only natural; smell is, <u>after-all,</u>[8] the most memorable sense for humans.

5. A. NO CHANGE
    B. poored over
    C. pour over
    D. pored over

6. F. NO CHANGE
    G. Beaches of Normandy
    H. beaches of Normandy
    J. Normandy's Beaches

7. A. NO CHANGE
    B. *Prejudice,* these books
    C. *Prejudice,* books
    D. *Prejudice* the books

8. F. NO CHANGE
    G. after all
    H. afterall
    J. after all,

9. Which sentence of paragraph 3 is antithetical to the intent of the passage?
    A. sentence 7
    B. sentence 8
    C. sentence 9
    D. sentence 10

(12) While very few people read reference books for fun, many researchers prefer paper <u>books versus online</u>[10] databases, which are usually inundated with pop-up windows and advertisements. (13) With books, readers can use paper bookmarks to easily compare several sources simultaneously. (14) Advanced publishing technology have shortened the time required to print new books, giving many reference books faster production cycles and making them easier to update frequently. (15) While some material may be more current on the Internet, the intricacies of computer-based research <u>were daunting</u>[12] for many researchers; the ability to make textual comparisons is circumscribed, and the problems of documenting source material are multiplied.

10. F. NO CHANGE
    G. books of online
    H. books from online
    J. books to online

11. Which choice best describes a grammatical error in sentence 14?
    A. subject-verb agreement error
    B. run-on sentence
    C. improper capitalization
    D. comma splice

12. F. NO CHANGE
    G. was daunting
    H. had been daunting
    J. can be daunting

(16) The peculiar relationship between writer and reader is best felt through the medium of a book. (17) A book, sometimes even a particular edition, casts a spell on the reader by which he or she <u>can literally explore</u>[13] the mind or heart of the author. (18) The relationship is apparent in the way that a child reads and deeply experiences a picture book, <u>to return to it</u>[14] repeatedly and treasuring the experience for years. (19) This experience melds the intellectual with the tactile, the cognitive with the emotional, and the personal with the universal; it is unique to the reader, the author, and the book that ties them together.

13. A. NO CHANGE
    B. literarily explore
    C. virtually explore
    D. explore

14. F. NO CHANGE
    G. returning to it
    H. to returning to it
    J. return to it

15. If one paragraph had to be deleted from this passage, which one could be deleted without affecting the author's main idea?
    A. paragraph 1
    B. paragraph 2
    C. paragraph 3
    D. paragraph 4

Vocabulary
Power Plus
for the
ACT
Vocabulary,
Reading, and Writing
Exercises for High Scores

Lesson Twenty

1. **echelon** (esh´ ə lon) *n.* a level of authority or responsibility; a rank
   Workers in the management *echelon* of the company were happy, but the laborers were about to go on strike.
   syn: level

2. **waive** (wāv) *v.* to relinquish something voluntarily; to refrain from enforcing
   Before testing the new medicine, he *waived* his right to sue the drug company.
   syn: forfeit; cede; defer   *ant: demand; enforce; impose*

3. **serendipity** (ser ən dip´ i tē) *n.* a knack or faculty of making fortunate discoveries by accident
   The discovery of penicillin is attributed to *serendipity* because the mold's properties were first observed when it was inadvertently allowed to contaminate a different experiment.
   syn: luck

4. **nondescript** (non di skript´) *adj.* lacking individual or distinct characteristics
   The private investigator drove a *nondescript* car so she could keep a low profile.
   syn: uninteresting; common; ordinary   *ant: unusual; unique; extraordinary*

5. **punitive** (pyōō´ ni tiv) *adj.* punishing; pertaining to punishment
   The government enacted *punitive* trade restrictions on any nation that refused to comply with new environmental laws.
   syn: disciplinary; corrective; retaliatory

6. **discerning** (di sûr´ ning) *adj.* having keen perception
   The *discerning* hunter spotted a deer hundreds of yards away.
   syn: perceptive; sharp; astute

7. **idyllic** (īdil´ ik) *adj.* simple and carefree; delightfully serene
   A hurricane ruined our plans for an *idyllic* vacation at the beach house.
   syn: charming; picturesque; pleasant   *ant: unpleasant; oppressive; dire*

8.   **acme**   (ak´ mē)   *n.*   the highest point
     Winning the championship game was the *acme* of the season.
     syn: pinnacle; climax; peak   *ant: nadir*

9.   **soluble**   (sol´ yə bəl)   *adj.*   easily dissolved
     The packets contain *soluble* powder for making iced tea.
                                                        ant: insoluble

10. **malinger**   (mə ling´ gər)   *v.*   to feign illness to avoid work
     Scott *malingered* so often that no one believed him when he was actually
     ill.
     syn: shirk

11. **cerebral**   (ser ə´ brəl)   *adj.*   favoring intelligence over emotions or instinct
     The dry novel had more a *cerebral* appeal than it had displays of drama.
     syn: intellectual; rational; logical   *ant: intuitive; instinctive*

12. **hypocrisy**   (hi pok´ ri sē)   *n.*   professing beliefs, feelings, or values that
        one does not have or practice
     In an act of complete *hypocrisy*, the actress who complains about the
     overuse of fossil fuels bought a second private jet.
     syn: insincerity; duplicity   *ant: sincerity; earnestness*

13. **conundrum**   (kə nun´ drəm)   *n.*   a difficult problem
     The police officer faced quite a *conundrum* when he caught his own son
     shoplifting.
     syn: quandary; predicament

14. **deleterious**   (del i tēr´ ē əs)   *adj.*   having a harmful effect; injurious
     Many people simply ignore the *deleterious* effects of prolonged exposure
     to the sun.
     syn: destructive; pernicious; damaging   *ant: beneficial; harmless; benign*

15. **relegate**   (rel´ i gāt)   *v.*   to place in an unfavorable place or position
     The tsar *relegated* his political enemies to the freezing tundra of Siberia.
     syn: demote; displace; exile

Exercise I

Words in Context

From the list below, supply the words needed to complete the paragraph. Some words will not be used.

soluble   echelon   punitive   waive
idyllic   discerning   deleterious

1.   The garage contained three generations of family junk, but Carla's _____ eye easily noticed the broken antique thermometer on the floor. She carefully picked it up, balancing the exposed blob of mercury on the top of the thermometer's tin backing. She knew that mercury fumes were _____ to good health, but she didn't realize that gold is _____ in liquid mercury until a drop of the substance dissolved a portion of her wedding ring. As she stared in disbelief at her ring, Carla easily thought of a few _____ chores for her son, who had knocked the old thermometer to the floor and then left to enjoy a[n] _____ summer day with his friends.

From the list below, supply the words needed to complete the paragraph. Some words will not be used.

cerebral   relegate   echelon   serendipity
conundrum   malinger   nondescript

2.   Newman faced a _____ at work. He had to inform the higher _____ that what began as a[n] _____ typographical error in the company's software was now threatening the stability of the entire company network; however, Newman himself was responsible for the error. He assumed that management, upon hearing the bad news, would _____ him to a demeaning job in the mail room, but to his surprise, the bosses were overjoyed that Newman had spotted the error before any major damage had been done. Newman decided not to inform them that his catch was a result of pure _____; he had found the error only because he had accidentally selected the wrong software to edit that day.

From the list below, supply the words needed to complete the paragraph. Some words will not be used.

acme	**malinger**	**cerebral**	**punitive**
hypocrisy	**nondescript**	**waive**	

3.   Tension at the civic association reached its _____ when Fred accused the governing council of _____. Fred claimed that the charter members _____ their own membership fees, and most of them _____ when the organization conducted activities that did not directly benefit its leaders. Council members accused Fred of making false accusations, but he said that it didn't take a[n] _____ giant to figure out that the leaders had been engaging in crooked practices.

Exercise II

Sentence Completion

Complete the sentence in a way that shows you understand the meaning of the italicized vocabulary word.

1.   The college might *waive* the requirement to take English 101 if you can prove that…

2.   A *discerning* collector will be able to…

3.   Sam, orphaned since the age of four, did not have the *idyllic*…

4.   The politician's *hypocrisy* became apparent when she made a speech about protecting wildlife and then approved…

5.   When the upper *echelon* of the company noticed Sandra's talent for eliminating unnecessary expenses, the board of directors decided to…

6.   In addition to fines and court costs, the company had to pay *punitive* damages meant to…

7.   Discovering the ancient treasure was the *acme* of…

8.   That car's leaking radiator is *deleterious* to…

9. After several disciplinary problems, Adam's parents decided to *relegate* their son to...

10. After an hour of reading the *cerebral* articles in the textbook, Matt just wanted to...

11. Sugar cubes are *soluble* in water, so if they get damp, they might...

12. The mechanic had to rely upon his own *serendipity* to fix the boat motor because...

13. Paul always *malingers* on days when...

14. The *nondescript* van outside looked like a common delivery truck, but it was actually...

15. The adventurers found themselves in a *conundrum* when they encountered...

Exercise III

Roots, Prefixes, and Suffixes

Study the entries and answer the questions that follow.

The root *pol* means "city."
The root *civ* means "citizen."
The root *urb* means "city."
The prefix *mega* means "large."
The prefix *sub* means "under."

1. Using literal translations as guidance, define the following words without using a dictionary.

    A. suburban   D. megalopolis
    B. civic   E. civilian
    C. urbanize   F. civil

2. The word *urbane* means "smooth," "polished," or "charming." Explain the possible reason for this word containing the root *urb*.

3. During a city council election, _____ might go door-to-door and ask you for your vote; however, if they refuse to leave your property, you might need to call the _____.

4. The prefix *metro* means "mother." What, literally, is a *metropolis*?

5. List as many words as you can think of that contain the prefix *sub*.

Exercise IV

Inference

Complete the sentences by inferring information about the italicized word from its context.

1. If Bill *waives* his rights of ownership in order to have his manuscript published, then he will not...

2. A person who prefers *cerebral* books about philosophy or science would probably not...

3. A scientist might attribute his or her success to *serendipity* if he or she did not intentionally...

Exercise V

Critical Reading

Below is a reading passage followed by several multiple-choice questions similar to the ones you will encounter on the ACT. Carefully read the passage and choose the best answer for each of the questions.

Socrates, one of the greatest philosophers in world history, was executed in 399 B.C. The passage recounts parts of Socrates' last speech before the judges of the Greek court condemned him to death.

FOR the sake of no long space of time, O Athenians, you will incur the character and reproach at the hands of those who wish to defame the city, of having put that wise man, Socrates, to death. For those who wish to defame you will assert that I am wise, tho I am not. If, then, you had waited for a short time, this would have

5 happened of its own accord; for observe my age, that it is far advanced in life, and near death. But I say this not to you all, but to those only who have condemned me to die. And I say this too to the same persons. Perhaps you think, O Athenians, that I have been convicted through the want of arguments, by which I might have persuaded you, had I thought it right to do and say anything so that I might escape

10 punishment. Far otherwise: I have been convicted through want indeed, yet not of arguments, but of audacity and impudence, and of the inclination to say such things to you as would have been most agreeable for you to hear, had I lamented and bewailed and done and said many other things unworthy of me, as I affirm, but such as you are accustomed to hear from others.

15 But neither did I then think that I ought, for the sake of avoiding danger, to do anything unworthy of a freeman, nor do I now repent of having so defended myself; but I should much rather choose to die having so defended myself than to live in that way. For neither in a trial nor in battle is it right that I or any one else should employ every possible means whereby he may avoid death; for in battle it

20 is frequently evident that a man might escape death by laying down his arms and throwing himself on the mercy of his pursuers. And there are many other devices in every danger, by which to avoid death, if a man dares to do and say everything.

But this is not difficult, O Athenians, to escape death, but it is much more difficult to avoid depravity, for it runs swifter than death. And now I, being slow

25 and aged, am overtaken by the slower of the two; but my accusers, being strong and active, have been overtaken by the swifter, wickedness. And now I depart, condemned by you to death; but they condemned by truth, as guilty of iniquity and injustice: and I abide my sentence and so do they. These things, perhaps, ought so to be, and I think that they are for the best.

30 In the next place, I desire to predict to you who have condemned me, what will be your fate: for I am now in that condition in which men most frequently prophesy, namely, when they are about to die. I say then to you, O Athenians, who have condemned me to death, that immediately after my death a punishment will overtake you, far more severe, by Jupiter, than that which you have inflicted on me.

35 For you have done this thinking you should be freed from the necessity of giving

an account of your life. The very contrary however, as I affirm, will happen to you. Your accusers will be more numerous, whom I have now restrained, though you did not perceive it; and they will be more severe, inasmuch as they are younger and you will be more indignant. For, if you think that by putting men to death you will
40 restrain any one from upbraiding you because you do not live well, you are much mistaken; for this method of escape is neither possible nor honorable, but that other is most honorable and most easy, not to put a check upon others, but for a man to take heed to himself, how he may be most perfect. Having predicted thus much to those of you who have condemned me, I take my leave of you.

45   But with you who have voted for my acquittal, I would gladly hold converse on what has now taken place, while the magistrates are busy and I am not yet carried to the place where I must die. Stay with me then, so long, O Athenians, for nothing hinders our conversing with each other, whilst we are permitted to do so; for I wish to make known to you, as being my friends, the meaning of that which has
50 just now befallen me. To me then, O my judges—and in calling you judges I call you rightly—a strange thing has happened. For the wonted prophetic voice of my guardian deity, on every former occasion, even in the most trifling affairs, opposed me, if I was about to do anything wrong; but now, that has befallen me which ye yourselves behold, and which any one would think and which is supposed to be
55 the extremity of evil, yet neither when I departed from home in the morning did the warning of the god oppose me, nor when I came up here to the place of trial, nor in my address when I was about to say anything; yet on other occasions it has frequently restrained me in the midst of speaking. But now it has never throughout this proceeding opposed me, either in what I did or said. What then do I suppose to
60 be the cause of this? I will tell you: what has befallen me appears to be a blessing; and it is impossible that we think rightly who suppose that death is an evil. A great proof of this to me is the fact that it is impossible but that the accustomed signal should have opposed me, unless I had been about to meet with some good.

                              [. . .]

65   You, therefore, O my judges, ought to entertain good hopes with respect to death, and to meditate on this one truth, that to a good man nothing is evil, neither while living nor when dead, nor are his concerns neglected by the gods. And what has befallen me is not the effect of chance; but this is clear to me, that now to die, and be freed from my cares, is better for me. On this account the warning in no
70 way turned me aside; and I bear no resentment toward those who condemned me, or against my accusers, although they did not condemn and accuse me with this intention, but thinking to injure me: in this they deserve to be blamed.

        Thus much, however, I beg of them. Punish my sons, when they grow up, O judges, paining them as I have pained you, if they appear to you to care for riches
75 or anything else before virtue, and if they think themselves to be something when they are nothing, reproach them as I have done you, for not attending to what they ought, and for conceiving themselves to be something when they are worth nothing. If ye do this, both I and my sons shall have met with just treatment at your hands.

        But it is now time to depart,—for me to die, for you to live. But which of us is
80 going to a better state is unknown to every one but God.

1. The best synonym for *incur,* as it is used in line 1, is
   A. enjoy.
   B. understand.
   C. avoid.
   D. experience.

2. In paragraph 1, Socrates asserts that he could have avoided punishment by
   F. defying his own conscience by telling his persecutors what they wanted to hear.
   G. providing better arguments despite his knowing that he is right.
   H. admitting that he is so aged that he is out of touch with Greek politics.
   J. arguing not with his persecutors but instead the general population.

3. As used in line 8, *want* most nearly means
   A. desire.
   B. lack.
   C. famine.
   D. choice.

4. According to paragraph 3, the accusers are guilty of
   F. theft.
   G. revenge.
   H. mercy.
   J. corruption

5. According to Socrates' argument in the second paragraph, his reluctance to talk his way out of punishment is analogous to
   A. using wisdom and logic to win over the loyalty of his oppressors.
   B. surrendering to superior forces in battle.
   C. fighting to the death instead of surrendering.
   D. judging others for words rather than actions.

6. An antonym for *depravity,* as Socrates uses the word in line 24, is
   F. sin.
   G. sloth.
   H. honor.
   J. shame.

7. Socrates is in the ideal time to prophesize, he contends, because he is
    A. thought insane.
    B. separated from society.
    C. on trial.
    D. near death.

8. The Greek counsel, according to Socrates in paragraph 4, can prevent civil upheaval only through
    F. subjugation of the most vocal freemen.
    G. execution of all critics.
    H. self reflection and moral improvement.
    J. understanding and respect.

9. Socrates demands that his sons be punished if they
    A. become government officials.
    B. take too much interest in wealth.
    C. refuse to attend their father's burial.
    D. do not follow the teachings of Plato.

10. The tone of the passage is best described as
    F. frustrated, but assertive.
    G. bold and optimistic.
    H. harsh and foreboding.
    J. resigned and defeated.

Vocabulary
Power Plus
for the **ACT**
Vocabulary,
Reading, and Writing
Exercises for High Scores

Lesson Twenty-One

1. **propinquity** (prə ping′ kwi tē) *n.* nearness; proximity
His *propinquity* to both murders made Tom a suspect.
syn: closeness; immediacy; adjacency   *ant: distance; remoteness*

2. **abrogate** (ab′ rə gāt) *v.* to abolish, especially by authority; to revoke formally
The town council voted to *abrogate* the unpopular law.
syn: annul; invalidate; repeal   *ant: establish; ratify; support*

3. **supine** (sōō pīn′) *adj.* lying on one's back; lying face-up
The hero lay helplessly *supine* in the villain's library after falling victim to the knockout gas.
       ant: prone

4. **prosaic** (prō zā′ ik) *adj.* straightforward and unimaginative; uninteresting
After missing my curfew, I had to sit through yet another boring, *prosaic* speech on family rules.
syn: banal; humdrum; monotonous   *ant: fascinating; inspiring*

5. **parity** (par′ i tē) *n.* equality
North and South Korea have no economic *parity*.
syn: balance; equivalence; proportion   *ant: disparity; imbalance*

6. **extrinsic** (ik strin′ sik) *adj.* not essential; extraneous
To make the aircraft lighter, the crew removed *extrinsic* parts not required for flight.
syn: unnecessary; adventitious   *ant: necessary; crucial; required; intrinsic*

7. **outré** (ōō trā′) *adj.* extremely unconventional; bizarre
Malcolm had an *outré* personality that made him well known for his odd behavior.
syn: eccentric; freaky; outlandish   *ant: conforming; ordinary*

8. **analects** (an′ ə lekts) *n.* selections from a literary work
The Eastern philosophy class discussed the *analects* of Confucius.

9. **surreptitious** (sûr əp tish´ əs) *adj.* accomplished through stealth and secrecy
    Smiling and nodding, the man cast a *surreptitious* glance at his watch while listening to his chatty neighbor.
    syn: furtive; sneaky; clandestine   *ant: open; candid*

10. **anomie** (an´ ə mē) *n.* societal or personal instability caused by a lack or erosion of values, standards, or ideals
    The Roman Empire ruled the world until widespread *anomie*, fueled by corruption, caused its decline.

11. **magniloquent** (mag nil´ ə kwənt) *adj.* lofty in expression; pompous
    In a *magniloquent* voice, the herald announced the arrival of the royal family.
    syn: grandiloquent; grandiose; ostentatious   *ant: humble; subtle; reserved*

12. **factotum** (fak tō´ təm) *n.* an employee with a variety of jobs or responsibilities
    As a *factotum* for the family business, Craig did the jobs of three employees.
    syn: workhorse; operator   *ant: principal*

13. **cognizant** (kăg´ nə zənt) *adj.* fully informed; having knowledge of
    Ben nodded his head, pretending to be *cognizant* of what the teacher was talking about.
    syn: aware; perceptive; sentient   *ant: ignorant; unaware; oblivious*

14. **febrile** (fe´ brīl) *adj.* pertaining to fever; feverish
    The *febrile* child was sent home from school to recover.

15. **apostasy** (ə păs´ tə sē) *n.* abandonment of one's principles, faith, or religious beliefs
    Government officials doubted the genuineness of the former spy's sudden *apostasy*.
    syn: defection; disavowal; renunciation   *ant: commitment; dedication; loyalty*

Exercise I

Words in Context

From the list below, supply the words needed to complete the paragraph. Some words will not be used.

outré	prosaic	propinquity	analects
surreptitious	cognizant	supine	

1. None of the guards noticed Alistair's _____ entry into the secret compound. The investigative reporter, known for his _____ strategies in obtaining information, had ridden through the gates beneath a supply truck, and now he lay _____ on the ground beneath the vehicle, searching for potential hiding places. He grimaced when he became _____ of the anthill directly beneath his shoulders, but he made no sound because of the _____ of the guards in front of the truck.

From the list below, supply the words needed to complete the paragraph. Some words will not be used.

factotum	cognizant	prosaic	extrinsic
magniloquent	parity	abrogate	

2. When the government _____ the use of clandestine agents as assassins and saboteurs, the CIA was forced to find new methods of dealing with foreign threats and interests. Mr. Bell was one of those methods. According to his personnel file, Mr. Bell was simply a "program manager" at the Pentagon; however, despite the bland job title, he was one of many _____ whose duty was to resolve those international problems that simple, public diplomacy cannot solve.

    Mr. Bell, whose real name is known only to his employer, gained most of his experience during the Cold War, when his primary mission was to ensure that the United States maintained defensive _____ with the Soviet Union. The work did include rare moments of extreme stress, but, to the disappointment of spy-thriller movie fans, the job most often involved hours of reading _____ logistics documents, most of which contained only _____ information that had little bearing on national security.

From the list below, supply the words needed to complete the paragraph. Some words will not be used.

supine	analects	febrile	magniloquent
parity	anomie	apostasy	

3.   Pete regretted his _____ from the simple life and desires he had before the massive failure of his dot-com endeavor. Like many other young entrepreneurs, Pete had allowed _____ to overtake him as he fixated on his monthly profit margins and failed to invest in advertising or customer service. Now he was bankrupt, and he watched as movers carried his _____ dining room furniture out the door of his house to the waiting moving truck and eventually to a public auction.

At moments, Pete's anger over his own poor judgment made him red-faced and _____, but he quickly recovered when he thought of a new marketing idea: he would create a best-selling novel that featured the personal accounts of the hundreds of failed dot-com business owners. The _____ of the failed owners would be excellent guidance for inexperienced entrepreneurs, like Pete, and also for investors.

Exercise II

Sentence Completion

Complete the sentence in a way that shows you understand the meaning of the italicized vocabulary word.

1. Madeline grew weary of being a *factotum* with the responsibilities of...

2. There is little *parity* in the quality of the hotel rooms; one room might look clean and new, while another room...

3. Detective Stone of the white-collar crimes division never understood the *apostasy* that caused successful people with wonderful families to...

4. Young Ralphie looked *febrile* this morning, so his mother...

5. As soon as the iron filings are in *propinquity* to the magnet, they...

6. Bored after sitting in the waiting room for an hour, Lenny picked up a *prosaic* pamphlet about...

7. Fiction and movies often depict the American Wild West as a place of *anomie*, where bounty hunters had routine gunfights with outlaws, and inhabitants could not rely on laws to...

8. The camper was not *cognizant* of the rattlesnake in her tent until...

9. The man's *outré* sales pitch involved the use of...

10. The English teacher said that the *extrinsic* information in the essay merely...

11. It took the spy five years to earn the *surreptitious* cover of...

12. When a passing policeman saw customers in the bank lying *supine*, he knew that...

13. Derek's parents *abrogated* his access to the computer after...

14. The students discussed *analects* from *The Adventures of Huckleberry Finn* while studying...

15. The narrator of the automobile commercial explained in a *magniloquent* voice why the featured car was...

Exercise III

Roots, Prefixes, and Suffixes

Study the entries and answer the questions that follow.

The roots *cur* and *curs* mean "to run."
The root *ambul* means "to walk."
The prefix *ob* means "in the way of" or "against."
The prefix *per* means "through."

1. Using literal translations as guidance, define the following words without using a dictionary.

   A. current
   B. ambulatory
   C. cursive

   D. amble
   E. occur
   F. perambulate

2. In the sentence, "John made a *cursory* inspection of his luggage," does the word *cursory* mean "fast," or "slow"?
   Explain why the blinking prompt on the display of a computer screen is called a *cursor*.

3. The root *somn* means sleep. If a person *somnambulates,* what is he or she doing?

4. A *current* is a flowing of something, or a passing from one person to another, so it is appropriate that coin or paper money, which circulates among people, is called _____.

5. List as many words as you can think of that contain the prefix *ob.*

Exercise IV

Inference

Complete the sentences by inferring information about the italicized word from its context.

1. If a religious sect experiences widespread *apostasy,* then members are probably...

2. In a household with many children, *parity* of parental attention might be difficult to maintain because...

3. The government might be forced to *abrogate* an unpopular law if...

Exercise V

Writing

Here is a writing prompt similar to the one you will find on the writing portion of the ACT.

How much money did you pay to attend your last baseball or football game? Add the costs of tickets, transportation, food, and souvenirs, and you're probably well into the hundreds of dollars—and all for the privilege of watching millionaires play games. The average salary of major league baseball players is presently over $3,000,000 annually.

Gladiators in the ancient Roman Empire—the first stadium stars—put their lives on the line for entertainment (not willingly, of course). Civil servants who risk their lives or help those everyone else has given up on earn modest salaries, typically. Why, then, do we enable sports figures, many of whom sit on the bench for a season, to make salaries worth tens of millions of dollars?

We live in a free-enterprise society, in which demand dictates price. It is true that we often reward talent and skill, but is a talent for catching a football on par with a talent for neurosurgery or caring for the terminally ill? Obviously, enough people are willing to pay the astronomical costs of professional sports for entertainment, but does that make it a worthy or justifiable expense? Should our culture be spending less on entertainment and more on education, medical care, poverty, or human rights?

Decide whether the cost of professional sports is acceptable. Take a position on the topic and write a letter to the editor of your local newspaper. Identify your stance, argue for or against the present situation, and offer your idea of a solution, or correction, to whatever you perceive as a problem. Support your argument with at least three subtopics.

Thesis: Write a one-sentence response to the above assignment. Make certain this sentence offers a clear statement of your position.

Example: In a free society, it is up to the individual to decide how much to pay for entertainment, and if people want to part with large amounts of their own money for the enjoyment of watching sports, it is entirely and acceptably their personal choice.

_____

_____

Organizational Plan: If your thesis is the point on which you want to end, where does your essay need to begin? List the points of development that are inevitable in leading your reader from your beginning point to your end point. This list is your outline.

1. _____

2. _____

3. _____

Draft: Use your thesis as both your beginning and your end. Following your outline, write a good first draft of your essay. Remember to support all of your points with examples, facts, references to reading, etc.

Review and revise: Exchange essays with a classmate. Using the Holistic scoring guide on page 245, score your partner's essay (while he or she scores yours). If necessary, rewrite your essay to correct the problems indicated by the essay's score.

Exercise VI

English Practice

Identifying Sentence Errors
Identify the errors in the following sentences. Choose the answer that fixes the error.
If the sentence contains no error, select NO CHANGE.

1. Concerned over the weather, Malcolm went outside and closed the windows of his car.
    A. NO CHANGE
    B. Concerned over the weather Malcolm went outside and closed the windows of his car.
    C. He was concerned over the weather, so Malcolm went outside and closed the windows of his car.
    D. Malcolm went outside, concerned over the weather, and closed the windows of his car.

2. United against all forms of tyranny, war seemed to us to be the only option.
    F. NO CHANGE
    G. United against all forms of tyranny, the only option seemed to be war.
    H. Only war seems to be the option, as we are united against all forms of tyranny.
    J. Since we were united against all forms of tyranny, war seemed to us to be the only option.

3. We need to make a decision about which of the three plans is more advantageous.
    A. NO CHANGE
    B. has more advantages.
    C. is most advantageous.
    D. is mostly advantageous.

4. Any student whose average is above a 90 will not need to take the final exam.
    F. NO CHANGE
    G. Any students, whose average is above a 90, will not need to take the final exam.
    H. All students who scored above a 90, will not need to take the final exam.
    J. Any student who's average is above a 90 will not be required to take the final exam.

5. The attendees at the concerned scientist's conference held its annual fund-raising meeting last week.
    A. NO CHANGE
    B. The attendees at the concerned scientist's conference held their annual fund-raising meeting last week.
    C. The attendees at the concerned scientists' conference held their annual fund-raising meeting last week.
    D. The attendees at the concerned scientists' conference held its annual fundraising meeting last week.

Improving Sentences
The underlined portion of each sentence below contains some flaw. Select the answer
that best corrects the flaw.

6. If the boys had been in the shed, <u>they would not hear the loud explosion,
    but since they were in the yard, they did notice the noise.</u>
    F. they could not hear the loud explosion, but since they were in the
        yard, they didn't notice the noise.
    G. they would not have heard the loud explosion, but since they were
        in the yard, they did notice the noise.
    H. they would not hear the loud explosion; since they were in the yard,
        they noticed the noise.
    J. they were unable to have heard the loud explosion, but since they
        were in the yard, they did notice the noise.

7. Many people believe <u>that the reason dinosaurs became extinct is because</u>
    the Earth's climate changed.
    A. that the reason the dinosaurs went extinct is because
    B. the reason dinosaurs became extinct is
    C. that dinosaurs became extinct when
    D. that dinosaurs became extinct because

8. <u>The court ruled that between the three candidates, the victor needs to
    receive the majority of the votes cast, not necessarily the plurality.</u>
    F. Among the three candidates, no one achieved a majority of the votes,
    G. The court ruled that between the three candidates, the victor needs
        to receive a plurality of the votes cast, not necessarily the majority.
    H. The court ruled that among the three candidates, the victor needs to
        receive a majority of the votes cast, not necessarily the plurality.
    J. The court ruled that among the three candidates, the victor needs to
        receive a plurality of the votes cast, not necessarily the majority.

9. Either the twins, the triplets, or the baby <u>have won the prize for being the
    most beautiful child in the contest.</u>
    A. has won the prize of the most beautiful child in the contest.
    B. has won the prize for being the most beautiful child in the contest.
    C. has won the prize for the most beautiful child in the contest.
    D. wins the prize for being the most beautiful child in the contest.

10. <u>So cold that his fingers would not move, a fire could not be built because
    the match was not able to be struck by the prospector.</u>
    F. The cold fingers of the prospector were unable to build a fire by
        striking the matches.
    G. So cold were the prospector's fingers that he could not build a fire
        by striking a match
    H. The prospector's cold fingers were unable to strike the match, thus
        leaving him unable to build the fire.
    J. The prospector's fingers were so cold that he could not strike a
        match to build a fire.

REVIEW
Lessons 15–21

Exercise I

Sentence Completion

Choose the best pair of words to complete the sentence. Most choices will fit grammatically and will even make sense logically, but you must choose the pair that best fits the idea of the sentence.

1. The _____ had a talent for turning news of _____ offenses into calamities that made headline news.
   A. tyro, tutelary
   B. pundit, venial
   C. schism, nondescript
   D. anomie, ascetic
   E. scion, soluble

2. The drunk driver was ordered to pay _____ damages for the emotional trauma of his victims in addition to _____ for the destruction of the victims' property.
   A. mutable, vicissitude
   B. surreptitious, analects
   C. alimentary, jurisprudence
   D. punitive, remuneration
   E. extant, encomium

3. Because of their _____ lifestyle of constant migration, the nomads carried only _____ items, essential for survival but light enough to travel with.
   A. ethereal, malevolent
   B. peripatetic, utilitarian
   C. extrinsic, idyllic
   D. arcane, spurious
   E. chthonian, transient

4. Because the medical staff moved with _____ after discovering the tumor, the patient is exhibiting _____ signs of recovery.
   A. impunity, tremulous
   B. propriety, cerebral
   C. parity, congenital
   D. jurisprudence, tangential
   E. celerity, propitious

5. Though the scientist was never exposed to high levels of radiation, the _____ dose he acquired during forty years of research proved to have _____ effects on his health.
   A. cumulative, deleterious
   B. mutable, discerning
   C. febrile, inchoate
   D. salubrious, trite
   E. stentorian, prominent

6. The secret spy network enjoyed complete _____ most of the time, except when critical missions required the approval of the upper _____ of leadership.
   A. serendipity, paladins
   B. parity, analects
   C. appellation, factotums
   D. autonomy, echelons
   E. vicissitude, scions

7. At the height of his _____, the washed-up star _____ for weeks on end, sleeping in a filthy condo surrounded by empty liquor bottles, strangers, and drug paraphernalia.
   A. impunity, relegated
   B. propinquity, coagulated
   C. depravity, dissipated
   D. nascent, waived
   E. exhilaration, rescinded

8. The FBI refused to allow the agent-in-training to _____ until it learned whether the allegations uncovered during the background investigation were genuine or _____.
   A. attenuate, fulsome
   B. matriculate, spurious
   C. malinger, prosaic
   D. exculpate, discerning
   E. satiate, indefeasible

Exercise II

Crossword Puzzle

Use the clues to complete the crossword puzzle. The answers consist of vocabulary words from lessons 15 through 21.

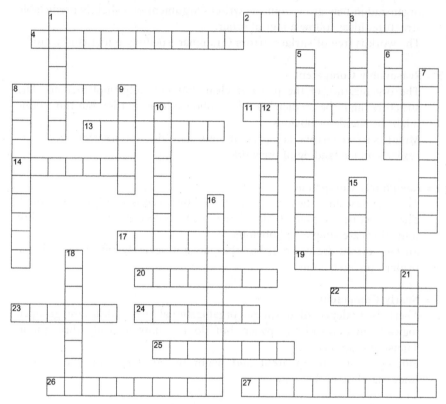

Across

2. moral corruption
4. compensation; payment
8. overused; hackneyed
11. name or title
13. employee with various duties
14. a level of authority; rank
17. to eradicate
19. descendant; heir
20. swiftness in action; speed
22. easily excused
23. equality
24. to suppress
25. formal praise
26. promising; auspicious
27. nearness

Down

1. to repeal
3. undeveloped
5. contemptuous; arrogant
6. lying face-up
7. difficult problem
8. digressing from the main point
9. known by only a few
10. very moving; touching
12. punishing
15. offensively flattering
16. unnecessary; excessive
18. to feign illness to avoid work
21. coming into existence

Scoring Guide for the ACT Writing Test

ORGANIZATION

6 = Clearly Competent

The paper is clearly organized around the central point or main idea. The organization may grow from the writer's argument or a slightly predictable structure. Ideas follow a logical order.

The work is **free of surface errors** (grammar, spelling, punctuation, etc.).

5 = Reasonably Competent

The organization of the paper is clear, but not fully implemented. The structure might be predictable. Ideas follow a logical order, but transitions might be simple or obvious.

Minor surface errors are present, but they **do not interfere** with the reader's understanding of the work.

4 = Adequately Competent

The organization of the paper is apparent, but not consistently implemented. The structure is predictable. Some ideas follow a logical order, but transitions are simple and obvious.

Surface errors are present, but they **do not severely interfere** with the reader's understanding.

3 = Nearly Competent

There is evidence of a simple organizational plan. Ideas are grouped logically in parts of the paper, but do not flow logically throughout. Transitions are needed.

Surface errors are **apparent** and **begin to interfere** with the reader's understanding of the work.

2 = Marginally Incompetent

The organizational plan of the paper is obscured by too few details and/or irrelevant details. Some of the ideas are grouped logically in parts of the paper. Transitions are needed or are incorrect.

Surface errors are **frequent and severe enough** to **interfere** with the reader's understanding of the work.

1 = Incompetent

There is no clear organizational plan and/or insufficient material. Ideas are not grouped logically. Transitions are absent.

Surface errors are **frequent** and **extreme,** and **severely interfere** with the reader's understanding of the work.

Scoring Guide for the ACT Writing Test

DEVELOPMENT

6 = Clearly Competent

The **paper takes a position** on the issue and **offers sufficient material** (details, examples, anecdotes, supporting facts, etc.) to create a **complete discussion. Every word and sentence is relevant.** Ideas are **fully supported.** The paper visits **different perspectives** of the argument or addresses **counterarguments** to the writer's position. The paper **focuses** on the argument evoked by the prompt. There is a **clear, purposed**, well developed **introduction** and **conclusion.**

The work is **free of surface errors** (grammar, spelling, punctuation, etc.).

5 = Reasonably Competent

The essay **takes a position** on the issue and **offers sufficient material** for a complete discussion, but the reader is left **with a few unanswered questions.**

Ideas are **supported.** The paper **partially visits different perspectives** of the argument or addresses **counterarguments.** Most of the paper **focuses** on the argument evoked by the prompt. There is **no irrelevant material.** There is a clear **introduction** and **conclusion.**

Minor surface errors are present, but they **do not interfere** with the reader's understanding of the work.

4 = Adequately Competent

The paper **takes a position** on the issue but **does not provide** enough details, examples, or supporting facts for a complete discussion, leaving a **few unanswered questions.** The paper includes **some attention** to **counterarguments** and differing perspectives. **Irrelevant material** is present. **Most** of the paper **focuses** on the topic and the specific argument. **Surface errors** are present, but they **do not severely interfere** with the reader's understanding.

3 = Nearly Competent

The essay **takes a position** on the issue but **does not include** sufficient details, examples, or supporting facts for a discussion. The paper **may include incomplete or unclear counterarguments.** The paper **might repeat** details or rhetoric. The paper focuses on the topic, but **does not maintain** the specific argument.

Surface errors are **apparent** and **begin to interfere** with the reader's understanding of the work.

2 = Marginally Incompetent

The paper **may not take a position** on the issue, or the paper may take a position but **fail to support** it with sufficient details. Examples and ideas are **vague** and **irrelevant**. The paper might **repeat ideas extensively**. The paper **might maintain focus** on the general topic.

Surface errors are **frequent and severe enough** to **interfere** with the reader's understanding of the work.

1 = Incompetent

The paper **might attempt to take a position**, but it **fails to provide** examples, fact, or rhetoric to support the position. The paper may be **repetitious** with **little** or **no focus** on the general topic.

Surface errors are **frequent** and **extreme**, and **severely interfere** with the reader's understanding of the work.

Scoring Guide for the ACT Writing Test

SENTENCE FORMATION AND VARIETY

6 = Clearly Competent

Sentences are **varied**, **complete**, and **assist the reader** in the flow of the discussion.

The work is **free of surface errors** (grammar, spelling, punctuation, etc.).

5 = Reasonably Competent

Sentences are **somewhat varied**, **generally correct**, and **do not distract** the reader from the flow of the discussion.

Minor surface errors are present, but they **do not interfere** with the reader's understanding of the work.

4 = Adequately Competent

Some sentences show **variety**, and **most** are **complete** and **generally correct**.

Surface errors are present, but they **do not interfere** with the reader's understanding.

3 = Nearly Competent

Sentences show a **little variety**, but the structure may be **dull**. Sentences are **generally complete** and grammatically correct, but **some errors** distract the reader.

Surface errors are **apparent** and **begin to interfere** with the reader's understanding of the work.

2 = Marginally Incompetent

Sentence Structure is usually simple. Problems in sentence structure and grammar distract the reader and provide little or no variety.

Surface errors are **frequent and severe enough** to **interfere** with the reader's understanding of the work.

1 = Incompetent

Sentence structure is **simple, generally erroneous** and **lacks variety**.

Surface errors are **frequent** and **extreme**, and **severely interfere** with the reader's understanding of the work.

Scoring Guide for the ACT Writing Test

WORD CHOICE

6 = Clearly Competent
The essay shows a **good command** of language. Word choice is **specific, clear**, and **vivid**, favoring **powerful nouns** and **verbs** to weaker adjective and adverb phrases. **Clear, specific words** are used, instead of vague, general terms.
The work is **free of surface errors** (grammar, spelling, punctuation, etc.).

5 = Reasonably Competent
Language is **competent**. Word choice is **clear** and **accurate**. Words and phrases are **mostly** vivid, specific, and powerful.
Minor surface errors are present, but they **do not interfere** with the reader's understanding of the work.

4 = Adequately Competent
Language is **adequate**, with **appropriate** word choice. **Most** words and phrases are vivid, specific, and powerful.
Serious surface errors are present, but they **do not interfere** with the reader's understanding.

3 = Nearly Competent
Language shows a **basic control** and word choice is **usually appropriate** but **inconsistent**.
Surface errors are **apparent** and **begin to interfere** with the reader's understanding of the work.

2 = Marginally Incompetent
Word choice is usually **vague**.
Surface errors are **frequent** and **severe enough** to **interfere** with the reader's understanding of the work.

1 = Incompetent
Word choice is **simple**, **vague**, and **inexact**. The writer makes **no attempt** to choose the best words for the topic, audience, and purpose.
Surface errors are **frequent** and **extreme**, and **severely interfere** with the reader's understanding of the work.

Scoring Guide for the ACT Writing Test

HOLISTIC

6 = Clearly Competent

The paper is **clearly organized** around the central idea. Ideas follow a **logical order**.

The paper **takes a position** on the issue and **offers sufficient material** (details, examples, anecdotes, supporting facts, etc.) to create a complete discussion. There is a **clear, purposed, well developed** introduction and conclusion.

The paper visits **different perspectives** of the argument or addresses **counterarguments** to the writer's position.

Sentences are **varied, complete**, and **assist the reader** in the flow of the discussion.

The paper shows a **good command** of language. Word choice is **specific, clear**, and **vivid**, favoring **powerful nouns** and **verbs** to weaker adjective and adverb phrases.

The work is **free of surface errors** (grammar, spelling, punctuation, etc.).

5 = Reasonably Competent

The organization of the paper is **clear**, but **not fully implemented**. Ideas follow a **logical order**, but transitions **might be simple** or obvious. The structure **might be predictable**.

The paper **takes a position** on the issue and **offers sufficient material** for a complete discussion, but the reader is left with **a few unanswered questions**. There is a clear **introduction** and **conclusion**.

The paper visits **some different perspectives** of the argument or addresses **counterarguments**.

Sentences are **somewhat varied, generally correct**, and **do not distract** the reader from the flow of the discussion.

Language is **competent**. Words and phrases are **mostly vivid, specific, and powerful**.

Minor surface errors are present, but they **do not interfere** with the reader's understanding of the work.

4 = Adequately Competent

The organization of the paper is **apparent**, but **not consistently** implemented. The structure is **predictable**. **Some** ideas follow a **logical order**, but transitions are **simple** and **obvious**. **Most** of the paper **focuses** on the topic and the specific argument.

The paper **takes a position** on the issue, but **does not provide** the details, examples, or supporting facts for a complete discussion, leaving **a few unanswered questions**.

The paper includes **little attention** to counterarguments and differing perspectives.

Irrelevant material is present.

Language is **adequate**, with appropriate word choice. **Most** words and phrases are vivid, specific, and powerful.

Some sentences show **variety**, and **most** are **complete** and **generally correct**.

Surface errors are present, but they **do not interfere** with the reader's understanding.

3 = Nearly Competent

There is **evidence of a simple organizational plan**. The essay **takes a position** on the issue but **does not include** sufficient details, examples, or supporting facts for a discussion. Ideas are **grouped logically** in parts of the paper, **but do not flow** logically throughout. The paper **focuses** on the topic, but **does not maintain** the specific argument.

The paper **may include incomplete** or **unclear** counterarguments.

Language shows a **basic control**, and word choice is **usually appropriate** but **inconsistent**. Sentences show a **little variety**, but the structure may be **dull**.

Sentences are **generally complete** and **grammatically correct**, but some errors **distract** the reader.

The paper might **repeat** details or rhetoric.

Surface errors are **apparent** and **begin to interfere** with the reader's understanding of the work.

2 = Marginally Incompetent

The organizational plan of the paper is **obscured by too few details** and/or **irrelevant details**. The paper **may not take a position** on the issue, or the paper may take a position but **fail to support** it with sufficient details. **Some** of the ideas are **grouped logically** in parts of the paper. The paper **generally maintains focus** on the general topic.

Examples and ideas are **vague** and **irrelevant**.

Sentence structure is **usually simple. Problems** in sentence structure and grammar **distract** the reader and provide **little** or **no variety. Word choice** is usually **vague**.

The paper might **repeat** ideas **extensively**.

Surface errors are **frequent and severe enough** to **interfere** with the reader's understanding of the work.

1 = Incompetent

There is **no clear organizational plan** and/or **insufficient material**. The paper **might attempt** to **take a position**, but it **fails** to provide examples, fact, or rhetoric to support the position. Ideas are **not grouped logically**.

The paper may be **repetitious** with little or **no focus** on the general topic.

Sentence structure is **simple** and **generally erroneous** and **lacking variety**. Word choice is **simple, vague**, and **inexact**. The writer makes **no attempt** to choose the best words for the topic, audience, and purpose.

Surface errors are **frequent** and **extreme**, and **severely interfere** with the reader's understanding of the work.

Relevant State Standards

<u>**Vocabulary Power Plus for the ACT – Book Four**</u>

High School - Grade 12

These are only the minimum standards that the product line meets; if these standards seem out of order, they typically go in "keyword" order; from the Language Usage category of standards, to Comprehension, Analysis, Writing, Research/Applied, and Technology/Media categories. Therefore these standards may be in a different order than the order given by your local Department of Education. Also if one state standard meets multiple categories, that particular standard is listed the first time it appears, to reduce redundancy. Again, please refer to your local Department of Education for details on the particular standards.

Bias/Validity standards are included, as is Voice/Style standards, as both categories include use of words for different effects on the audience (connotation, denotation, distortion, formality, etc.) and thus are logical inclusions.

Depending on state, standards pertaining to use of dialect and idiomatic expressions might be met by this product. Please refer to your local Department of Education for details.

Notation is as close as possible to the notation given by the Department of Education of the respective state.

States:

Alabama:
Std. 34; Std. 1; Std. 5; Stds. 24-28; Std. 29; Std. 9; Stds. 20-22; Std. 13; Std. 14; Std. 8; Std. 1; Std. 3; Std. 4; Std. 6; Std. 23

Alaska (GLEs only up to Grade 10; Grade 10 repeated here):
R4.1.1-4; R4.4.1-2; R4.5.1; R4.5.2-3; W4 (all); R4.1.5; R4.2.1-2; R4.3.1-4; R4.3.5-6; R4.7.1; R4.9.2; R4.9.1; R4.6.1-4; W4.2.2; W4.4.5

Arizona:
R1.4PO1-2; W3.3PO1; R1.5PO1; R2.1PO5; R2.1PO2-3; W1 (all); W2.4-6PO (all); W3 (all); R1.6PO1-5; R3.3PO2-3; R3.1PO4; VP-P1; R1.5PO1; R2.2PO1-3; R2.2PO3; W3 (entire)

Arkansas:
R.11.12.1-4; W.5.12.5; R.10.12.1; R.10.12.17; R.9.12.2; R.9.12.14; R.10.12.21; W.4.12 (all); W.6.12 (all); W.7.12 (all); W.5.12 (all); R.9.12.3; W.5.12.4; R.9.12.1; R.9.12.6; R.9.12.4; R.10.12.20; R.10.12.19; W.5.12.1; W.5.12 (entire); W.7.12.8

California:
R1.1-3; R2.2-5; R3.8-9; R2.1; W2.5; R3.3-4; WOC1.1-3; W1.1; W2 (all); R2.6

Colorado (broad standards):
S1; S6; S2; S3; S4

Connecticut:
1.3 (all); 1.1 (all); 2.1 (all); 1.2g; 3.2 (all); 4.2 (all); 3.1 (all); 1.4 (all); 2.3 (entire); 2.1D

Delaware:
2.2a; 1.5; 2.4k; 2.4bL; 4.2b; 2.4bI/T; 4.2c; 1.1; 1.3; 1.2; 1.1, 1.5; 2.4j; 2.5f; 4.3A; 2.4G; 2.3A,C

District of Columbia:
12.LD-V.8-9; 12.LT-F.6; 12.IT-DP.6-7; 12.LT-G.2; 12.LT-T.4; 12.LT-F.5; 12.W-R.5; 12.W-E.2-4; 12.W-I.1; 12.W-E.2-4; 12.LT-F.7; 12.LT-S.14; 12.LD-O.6

Florida (broad standards):
R.1 (all); R.2 (all); Li.1 (all); W.1 (all); W.2.3; La.1.2; LVS.1.4; Li.1.1; Li.1 and 2

Georgia:
ELA12RC3; ELA12RL5; ELA12RL1; ELA12W1; ELA12C1; ELA12RL4; ELA12W2; ELA12RL3; ELA12W4

Hawaii (broad standards):
S2; S1; S4; S5,6; S7; S3

Idaho:
12.LA.1.8.1-2; 12.LA.4.2.3; 12.LA.1.2.1; 12.LA.2.3.4-5; 12.LA.3 (all); 12.LA.5.4.1-2; 12.LA.4 (all); 12.LA.2.1.2-3; 9-12.Spch.6.3; 12.LA.2.1.1; 12.LA.4.2-4

Illinois:
1.A.5a-b; 1.C.5a-d, f; 2.B.5a-b; 1.B.5c; 3.C.5b; 1.B.5b; 2.A.5a; 3.A.5; 3.C.5a-b; 1.C.5e; 2.A.5C; 4.B.5C

Indiana:
12.1.1-3; 12.3.1; 12.3.3-4; 12.4.1-6, 10-11; 12.6 (all); 12.5 (all); 12.4.12; 12.2.1; 12.2.3, 5, 6; 12.5.9; 12.3.8-9; 12.3.5,7,10; 12.5.9

Iowa (Model Core Curriculum):
R6; R1; R3; W1; W7; W3; W2; R4; V3; R5; S7

Kansas:
RB3:1-3, 5; RB4:13; RB4:1; RB3:4; RB4:11; RB4:2-6, 9-10; RB4:14-15; LB1:2; LB2 (entire)

Kentucky (Academic Expectatiqns):
AE1.2; AE2.30, 33; AE2.38; AE1.11; AE6.1, 2.25

Louisiana:
RR1.1; RR7.9; W2.20; RR6.7; RR1.2; WP3 (all); W2.14-17, 20; W2.19; RR7.11; SL4.32; RR1.2; RR6.5-6; RR6.8; W2.17

Maine:
A1; B7; B8, D4; A6; E1-3; F1-3; G4-5; G8; C7-8; B5-6; B10-11; E1,4

Maryland (HAS documents used):
G3.2.2; G1.1.1-4; G1.1.5; G2.1 (all); G1.2.2-3; G3.1 (all); G3.3 (all); G2.1 (all); G1.3.3; G4.3.1; G2.3.3; G1.2.5; G1.2.4

Massachusetts:
4.26-27; 10.6; 14.6; 15.10; 21.9; 22.10; 5.30; 6.10; 19.28-30; 20.6; 8.34; 9.7; 8.32-33; 11.7; 25.6; 19.30

Michigan (Michigan Merit Curriculum);
3.3; 3.2; 1.1; 4.1; 1.3, 1.5; 2.1, 2.2; 2.3

Minnesota:
IB4-5; IB1-5; ID14; IC3; ID9; IC4; ID4-5; IIB1-8; IIC2-3; IIA1; IIC1; IIIB5-7, 9-10; IC8; ID15; ID1-3; ID4,10; ID12; IIIA7

Mississippi:
2a-d; 3f-g; 1a-d; 3a; 4a-c; 3b-e; 2e-f; 2D1

Missouri:
I5c; II2b; II11; I6a-d; II3c; IV2d; I1c; III1a; I1a; III1b; II4a, c-h; II6a-b; III1a; II3a-b; I3b-c; I3d; I5B; I4A,C; III1D

Montana:
RCS2; RCS1; LCS1; RCS5; WCS2; WCS1; WCS4; RCS4; LCS2; LCS5; RCS3

Nebraska (standards set at grade 12):
12.1.1; 12.1.5; 12.1.6

Nevada (standards set at grade 12):
1.12.3; 1.12.4-5; 2.12.1-3; 4.12.6; 5.12.2; 3.12.7; 3.12.5-6; 6.12.1-5, 7; 7.12.1-5; 5.12.2-6; 3.12.3; 3.12.1; 8.12.2

New Hampshire:
R-12-1, 2, 3; R-12-13; R-12-7.2; R-12-4.4; R-12-7.5; R-12-4.5; W-12-10; W-12-9; W-12-11.4; W-12-1.4; W-12-7.3; R-12-4.1-3; R-12-12.1; R-12-8.4; R-12-11.1-3; R-12-16.1

New Jersey:
3.1.F.1-3; 3.1.G.12-13; 3.2.D.6; 3.1.D.3; 3.2.B.1; 3.1.G.11; 3.1.G.6; 3.1.G.8; 3.2.A (all); 3.2.C (all); 3.2.B.5; 3.2.B.1; 3.2.D.2; 3.2.D.8; 3.1.E.1-3; 3.1.G.9; 3.1.H.6; 3.4.B.2-3; 3.5.B.1; 3.1.G.5; 3.1.G.3; 3.1.G.7; 3.2.A.6-7

New Mexico:
1D1; 1C2; 3A1-2; 1D5; 1B1-2; 1A3; C1; 1A1; 3B1; 1D2-3; 2D4; 1B3
New York (broad standards):
ELA-S1, ELA-S2; ELA-S3

North Carolina:
6.01; 4.01-02; 1.03, 4.03; 2.04; 6.02

North Dakota:
12.3.5; 12.3.1; 12.2.1; 12.2.2; 12.2.5-6; 12.6.3; 12.3.3-6, 8-11; 12.6.1; 12.3.2; 12.3.7; 12.2.3

Ohio:
12-WC; 12-RP; 12-RA-IT; 12-RA-L; 12-WP; 12-WC; 12-WA

Oklahoma:
12-RL1 (all); 12-RL2-1b; 12-RL3-1; 12-RL2-1a; 12-RL2-4c; 12-RL3-3; 12-WM1 (all); 12-WM3 (all); 12-WM2 (all); 12-RL2-1E; 12-RL2-2A; 12-RL3-2D-E; 12-RL2-4D; 12-WM1-6; 12-WM1-2; 12-WM1-6-7

Oregon: EL.CM.RE.02; EL.CM.LI.01; EL.CM.LI.11-14; EL.CM.LI.17-18; EL.CM. WR.07; EL.CM.WR.21-26

Pennsylvania (standards set at grade 11):
1.1.11C; 1.1.11E-F; 1.1.11G; 1.1.11H; 1.1.11B; 1.3.11C; 1.5.11 (all); 1.4.11 (all); 1.1.11D; 1.3.11C; 1.3.11B; 1.4.11D-E

Rhode Island:
R-12-1, 2, 3; R-12-13; R-12-7.2; R-12-4.4; R-12-7.5; R-12-4.5; W-12-10; W-12-9; W-12-11.4; W-12-1.4; W-12-7.3; R-12-4.1-3; R-12-12.1; R-12-8.4; R-12-11.1-3; R-12-16.1

South Carolina:
E4-R3.1-4; E4-W1.6.2, 4; E4-R1.3, 5; E4-R2.3, 5; E4-W1 (all); E4-R1.7-9; E4-R1.4; E4-C3.7; E4-R2.1; E4-R2.3,6; E4-R2.4; E4-W1.4; E4-W1.6.3; E4-W1.6

South Dakota:
12.W.1.1; 12.R.1.1, 12.R.2.1; 12.L.1.1; 12.W.2.1; 12.L.1.1; 12.R.3.1; 12.S.1.2; 12.W.1.1

Tennessee (Learning Expectations):
2LE-3; 2LE-1; 4LE-10; 1LE-1; 2LE-4, 5, 8; 2LE-13; 2LE-14; 1LE- 5-10; 1LE-11; 1LE-2, 3, 4; 2LE-10; 2.03-05; 2.06; 2.12; 2.09; 1.18; 1.01,02,05,06; 1.11

Texas (TEKS section 110.45):
b7 (all); b8 (all); b11 (all); b9 (all); b12E; b2 (all); b3 (all); b1 (all); b13 (all); b20C; B8I; B9D; B5D; B12G; B10C; B6 (entire); B1B-F

Utah:
1-O1 (all); 2-O3 (all); 2-O2 (all)

Vermont:
R-12-1, 2, 3; R-12-13; R-12-7.2; R-12-4.4; R-12-7.5; R-12-4.5; W-12-10; W-12-9; W-12-11.4; W-12-1.4; W-12-7.3; R-12-4.1-3; R-12-12.1; R-12-8.4; R-12-11.1-3; R-12-16.1

Virginia:
12.4 (all); 12.3a; 12.7 (all); 12.8b; 12.3 (entire); 12.2 (entire)

Washington (EALRs used here):
R1.2; R2 (all); R3 (all); W2.4; W1 (all); W3.3; W2 (all); W3.2; W4.1

West Virginia (prefix for these citations: RLA.O):
12.1.10; 12.1.04, 06, 09, 11; 12.2.01; 12.1.02; 12.1.05, 07; 12.2.08-13; 12.1.12; 12.1.01; 12.2.10

Wisconsin (standards set at grade 12):
D.12.1; A.12.1; A.12.4; A.12.2; B.12.2; B.12.3; B.12.1; A.12.2-3

Wyoming:
R-IB; R-IA; R-IIIB2; R-IIA; R-IIIA; R-IIC; W-IB; W-IE, F, G; W-IA; W-ID; R-IIIA2; SL-1b; R-IIB2,5; SL-9